Imagining Philadelphia

Imagining Philadelphia

TRAVELERS' VIEWS OF THE CITY
FROM 1800 TO THE PRESENT

PHILIP STEVICK

PENN

UNIVERSITY OF PENNSYLVANIA PRESS

PHILADELPHIA

Permission is acknowledged to reprint material from the following works:

Hollis Alpert. "Philadelphia: Plans and Pigeons." *Partisan Review*, vol. 17, no. 7 (1950). Courtesy of *Partisan Review* and the author.

Dizzie Gillespie. *To Be, or Not . . . to Bop*. Reprinted by permission of Doubleday and Co., Inc.

John Gunther. *Inside U.S.A.* Copyright © 1947, 1951 by John Gunther; renewed 1974, 1979 by Jane Perry Gunther. Reprinted by permission of Harper Collins Publishers, Inc.

John Lukacs. *Philadelphia: Patricians and Philistines, 1900–1950*. Copyright © 1981 by John Lukacs. Reprinted by permission of Farrar, Straus and Giroux, Inc.

Bruce Springsteen. "The Streets of Philadelphia." Courtesy of Jon Landau Management.

Gary Stoller. "The Friendly Cities." Copyright © 1994 by Condé Naste Publications, Inc. Courtesy of the *Condé Naste Traveler*.

Library of Congress Cataloging in Publication Data
Stevick, Philip.
    Imagining Philadelphia : travelers' views of the city from 1800 to the
present / Philip Stevick.
        p.   cm.
    Includes bibliographical references and index.
    ISBN 0-8122-3377-8 (alk. paper)
    1. Philadelphia (Pa.) – Description and travel.   2. Travelers – Pennsylva-
nia – Philadelphia.   I. Title.
F158.3.S74   1996   96-16520
917.48′ 11044 – dc20   CIP

To Abby

Contents

Illustrations

Acknowledgments

From the first time I saw it, Philadelphia seemed to me both intriguing and a little baffling. I found it natural to talk about the city with others who were in the city but not exactly of it. And all of those conversations about Philadelphia form a background for this book. I am grateful to many penetrating and observant friends who taught me, without meaning to, their ways of understanding the city.

More immediately, the writing of the book began with a Study Leave from Temple University. I am happy to thank my colleagues in the English Department and elsewhere in the university for thinking well of the idea of this book. Without a block of time away from customary duties, it would not have been written.

Some of the people who have been especially helpful to me are Joshua Cohen, Bob Eskind, Ken Finkel, Ed Fuller, Phil Lapsansky, Bruce Laverty, Sally Mitchell, Miles Orvell, Dan Stevick, Susan Stewart, Sarah Weatherwax, Tom Whitehead, and Alan Wilde.

Introduction

In 1828, Mrs. Anne Royall–journalist and editor, crusader, and observer of manners and morals–published the second of her travel accounts, *The Black Book: A Continuation of Travels in the United States*. Like the first, her *Sketches of History: Life and Manners in the United States by a Traveller*, it has a fairly random order to it, structured on her itinerary, of course, but otherwise loosely impressionistic, the impressions ranging from the acerbic to the ingenuous. In due course she visits Philadelphia.

It is people more than the sights of the city that draw her comments: she takes a vigorous pleasure in being impressed by the not-so-famous and finding some of the better known residents of the city more than a little banal. But of her several pages on Philadelphia, no single judgment carries a more luminous conviction than her enthusiastic endorsement–of Philadelphia peaches. Less than a page into her description of the city, she has discovered them: charming, she calls them, "charming peaches the largest and best I ever saw."[1]

Consider what she might have seen in the Philadelphia of 1828. Or, perhaps more precisely, consider what she probably saw but thought not worth commenting on. For a century the first city of North America in population and commerce, Philadelphia had lost its place to New York in the previous two decades. But there was a mature, elegant, comfortable quality to the city that seemed European to even casual visitors in a way that New York had not become–a shaded, lighted, poised, intelligible city, with a considerable range of cosmopolitan pleasures and an extraordinary variety of cultural institutions. Architecturally, the city in 1828 looked like no other: in addition to its basic mixture of brick, attached housing, the city had only recently begun to add its distinctive block-long rows of continuous, uniform houses, a Philadelphia innovation; and within a few years prior to 1828, some of the most striking public buildings in the country had been completed—Strickland's triumphant Second National Bank, for example. Any traveler's interest in Independence Hall, then the State House, would have been re-energized by the deaths of Thomas Jefferson and John Adams, both, by an amazing coincidence, on July 4, 1826, exactly fifty years after the ratification of the Declaration of Independence. There had been the mourning draperies, the muffled bell, the solemn memorial services at the State House, widely described in the national press; and no cultivated person would have forgotten it by 1828. Although it would not admit its first prisoner for another year, Eastern State Penitentiary, at the northern edge of the city, had been under construction for fifteen years: in 1828, it was already a frequent destination of visiting travelers, not only as the fulfillment of an extraordinary innovation in penal reform but as by far the most expensive building in the United States up to that time. And by the 1820s, the Fairmount Waterworks was in full operation, probably the most audacious work of engineering of the first quarter of the American century and a site so visually lovely that it was both the most visited and the most pictorially represented place within the city.

Why, in the face of so much to see, Mrs. Royall should have been so impressed with Philadelphia's peaches seems, at first, amusing and incomprehensible. Although it must have been possible to buy an excellent peach in Philadelphia at that time, there is, of course, no reason to suppose Philadelphia peaches superior to peaches bought, say, in Baltimore. Still, placing Mrs. Royall's eccentric observation against the ideal tour of Philadelphia that I have begun to sketch out—easy though it is to do—is both diversionary and irresponsible. It is not only a facile condescension to a woman of courage and wit who does not deserve to be patronized for not having seen the right things; it is, further, to mistake the nature of what people write when they travel.

Travelers see what they will, not what they are supposed to see. A hundred distractions of mood and circumstance can divert a traveler from one sight to another. And the plain quality of being interested is so mysterious and evanescent as to be beyond analysis. Travelers write about what they have seen because it gives them pleasure to do so, not because they wish to satisfy a reader over a century and a half in the future. Of course, some visiting writers seem to catch the spirit of a place better than others. But to some extent, all writers who report on being away from home notice the peaches rather than the waterworks. It is not only that travelers, like anybody else, are unique individuals. They all carry, in addition, an immense load of experiential and cultural baggage that disposes them to "read" a place in a particular way, to see things that are scarcely there, and to be unable to see other things, even though they may be staring straight at them. It is a truism to say that there is no Philadelphia apart from the individual perceptions of the people who have been there; or, to state the matter differently, there are as many Philadelphias as there are observers of the city.

Consider another example. Emerson traveled widely and visited Philadelphia several times. During the years of his maturity, he kept voluminous notebooks, and brief notations appear concerning the places he visited, Philadelphia among them. Most of the notebook entries are not very interesting. They are private and utilitarian: addresses, names of friends visited and lectures delivered, an unpolished fragment of wit, an aphorism. But on one occasion Emerson mentions Philadelphia, and an interested reader is likely to be brought up short by his observation. "In Philadelphia," he writes, "they play chess in all houses."[2] He goes on, in one more sentence, to describe a chess game played at the Athenaeum "at all hours." And then the observations on Philadelphia are done, leaving a reader without a clue concerning Emerson's strange leap of logic, from the observation of some chess players to the conclusion that everybody in Philadelphia played the game.

What Mrs. Royall and Emerson have in common is this, and perhaps nothing else: both of them passed through Philadelphia and recorded an observation that no one else before or since has made—that Philadelphia has charming peaches and that, in Philadelphia, everybody plays chess. Both events remind us of how idiosyncratic travel, and writing about it, really are. And both events suggest that visiting Philadelphia has always had about it a fluid, indeterminate quality, in contrast to other destinations its size, where the experience of a visit is likely to be more clearly defined and specific.

Some cities, especially older, more complicated cities, have a diverse and vivid collection of iconic images that are likely to precede anyone's visit there. By iconic I mean to suggest images that are both crisply visual and iterative: an ordinary person will have seen them and seen them again. If "iconic" suggests a mythic or quasi-religious aspect, then that is appropriate too: such images are highly charged, with symbolic power, awe, desire. Thinking about going to London, for example, a traveler easily imagines a dozen epitomizing places—Big Ben, the Tower Bridge, a Buckingham Palace Guard—the looks of which can be pictured quite clearly since they have been seen a hundred times, in books and magazines and in travel advertisements. Insofar as a journey to London has about it something of a pilgrimage, those iconic images are the objects of the quest. A traveler, expecting to visit New York, knows what the Brooklyn Bridge and the Flatiron Building look like before the trip has begun–the same holds true for Times Square, the Empire State Building, the Statue of Liberty. And each of those epitomizing images is likely to evoke a dimension of longing in the traveler. The traveler, arriving in New York, knows it is indeed New York because it is possible to manipulate one's field of vision so as to replicate the image held in the mind. Having seen Times Square on television on New Year's Eve, the traveler *sees* it and the result is a confirmation, a fulfillment, and a frisson.

Philadelphia is not like that. There have always been Independence Hall and later the Liberty Bell, both of them clear enough as images in the mind but neither very potent as destinations of the heart. Beyond those it is hard to know what would grip the imagination of anyone about to set out for the city. Fairmount Park, for example, is remarkable, and there is no city park system equal to it in size and variety. But it is not a picture in the mind of anyone living elsewhere and no one travels to Philadelphia to see it. It is not that the city lacks impressive things to see and do. Indeed the chapters that follow record the interest that two centuries of travelers have found in the city. It is, rather, that the city's quintessential images lack the kind of resonance that would haunt the consciousness of people living elsewhere so as to make specific their expectations of the visual experience of an actual visit.

Of the Philadelphia of 1900, John Lukacs contemplates the photographs of the period, taken from City Hall tower or any high building, showing "a brown sea of houses." Even when the photograph is black and white, it seems to contain "a sepia undertone." However one turns the picture or manipulates the perspective, the impression remains. "There is hardly a single landmark that would be recognizable to people who are not Philadelphians, not one outstanding building, not one particular vista," with the single exception of City Hall itself.[3]

So it is that Philadelphia is, to some extent, a carte blanche for the visitor. Travelers' reports are sometimes vague and ill-defined, as if it were difficult to understand a city whose reputation is so lacking in a kind of crisp pictorial concreteness before the fact. Sometimes travelers' reports are blandly predictable, as if the visitor lacked the will to define the city when so little particularity had preceded him. Sometimes those accounts are random and inscrutable, such as Mrs. Royall's and Emerson's. And sometimes they bring a creative, visionary quality to the experience of the city that seems, from our distance, extraordinary.

Within one kind of framework, the apposite questions about Philadelphia inquire, of course, into the stages of its growth and prosperity, its commerce and its institutions, its racial and ethnic tensions, its urban health; and the answers to those sensible and systematic questions can be found in the archives and the organizational and narrative art of the historians of the city. Within a different framework, the questions of how the city impressed itself upon visitors' imaginations, how they organized and valued the experience of the city, how they transformed it—these are the salient questions. The second framework, the city as an occasion for imaginatively constructing the idea of itself, is a parallel inquiry to the historians': the city is the same city, its streets run in the same directions, and the dates are the same. But the pertinence of the factual is quite different in the two.

Imagine that Mrs. Royall's observation had been extended, that she was equally impressed by the apples and pears, the cherries and plums, and that she found (as did others) that the oysters of the city were both numerous and succulent. A vision of the city would begin to take shape, Philadelphia as a kind of cornucopia of the Middle Atlantic states. The facticity of it all is rather beside the point, the city being bountiful enough to support such a vision and the deliciousness of the fruit being a matter beyond the domain of fact. Behind Emerson's observations on chess there surely lie some predispositions: he does not say enough to allow us to recover them. But the pertinence of fact is just as marginal as it is with Mrs. Royall's visit. It is surely not possible to discover the number of people in Philadelphia who played chess in mid-nineteenth century, but no one, reading Emerson's notation, would ever be inclined to try to find out. The observation of Emerson has only the slenderest connection with social history but has everything to do with the interaction between what seemed to be a leisured and gentle city and America's great nineteenth-century sage.

Occasionally a traveler to Philadelphia, who writes about it, is so explicit in intent, so precise in expectation, and so comparatively uncomplicated in mind and spirit that the imagining of the city seems perfectly clear and nonproblematic. An English clergyman, Henry Caswall, having been rector of a parish in Indiana for some ten years, decided to tour the United States with the purpose of reporting on the nature and the vitality of the American church; he published a narrative of his tour in 1839. True to his stated purpose, he subordinated every observation – of scenery and topography, institutions, social custom – to the larger intent of providing a judicious assessment of the Episcopal Church in America. Midway through his tour, he visited Philadelphia.

In a few sentences he has sketched in the setting, the population, and the temper of the city, all without much color or detail, seemingly without much interest. The city "contains some valuable public libraries, and many benevolent, scientific, and literary institutions." Done with the preliminaries, he settles into his subject.

There are at present thirty-three Episcopal clergymen in Philadelphia, and twelve churches, one of which, St. Thomas's, is designed for coloured persons. There are twice as many Presbyterian houses of worship, ten Quaker, and ten Methodist. Besides these there are nearly forty meeting-houses of various denominations, including six Roman Catholic churches and two synagogues. The rector of the Episcopal Church of St. Paul's reported, in 1836, 449 communicants, and 480 Sunday-scholars. The rector of St. Andrew's reported at the same time 361 communicants, 785 Sunday-scholars, and contributions during the past year to missionary and similar purposes amounting to 3506 dollars (789£). The entire number of Episcopalian worshippers in Philadelphia is probably 12,000 and of communicants, 3000.[4]

One only guesses that the Reverend Caswall knew the multitude of attractions to be found in the second city of the Republic. But he renders Philadelphia as a city of churches. And all of the energy and diversity of the city are distilled into the single matter of its Christian worship. Sober and pious and systematic though it is, Caswall's grip on the city is as odd as Mrs. Royall's and Emerson's.

Such highly individual impressions of the city as the Reverend Caswall's, and Emerson's and Mrs. Royall's, never lose their power to captivate, whether because of their single-mindedness or their sheer perversity. But the versions of Philadelphia that seem most engaging, most plainly interesting for our century, contain two simultaneous levels of response to the city. One is a tangible, sensory immersion in the life of the physical city, a sense, however fragmentary, that Philadelphia was really visited, at street level, on a specific time during a particular journey. The other level is a mythic, transformative response, in which a visit to Philadelphia becomes the occasion for a play of mind, a complex act of the imagination, so that the scene of the city, as caught in the memory and held on the page, contains qualities that seem visionary perhaps, even dreamlike, a sustained construction with a highly personal tilt to it; and the report of the visit becomes fictive in the highest and best sense, an invention, something "made up," answerable, in some mysterious way, to the laws of its own construction.

More than a century after those travelers of the 1820s and 1830s, the *Saturday Evening Post* ran a series called "Cities of America," later gathered as a book, written by George Sessions Perry, a prominent feature writer of the period. The essay on Philadelphia, of course, addresses a city vastly altered in the intervening years, heavily industrialized, expanded, and consolidated, with a population in its metropolitan area ten times larger. Whatever his background, Perry describes the city as an outsider, a clever and knowing visitor, not a resident, and the pronouns establish his subject as "Philadelphians-they," not "Philadelphians-we." Written in a confident, magisterial style, never ambivalent, never hesitant in the face of complexity, given to broad strokes of colorful generality, the essay lays out its controlling images at its beginning.

There are two fairly distinct Philadelphias. One is the ghost, the living legend of a great and dynamic city which, among other things, founded this free nation. Many of the physical evidences of that stately old city remain, so many indeed that, though its spunky spirit has long since withered and vanished, it can be clearly recaptured in a sensible, tactile way.

The other Philadelphia, the contemporary one, is the sprawling, and in some ways backward, city that occupies the location of its distinguished predecessor.[5]

Multiplex though the city may be, Perry resolves his response to it into an antithesis. Philadelphia is engaging and dilapidated, charming and shabby, once vital, now complacent, once daring, now lethargic.

In our time, fifty years later, it may well be not so much its central images and their thematic import that seem striking so much as Perry's tone. There is a jaunty congeniality throughout: As if it were a ship, the city is feminized—"She has certain natural advantages . . . "; Benjamin Franklin, in time, comes to be as "handy" to his adopted city "as a pocket in a shirt"; Andrew Jackson is "Andy." And the city is sometimes personified: "Philadelphia is a city that wears a cutaway coat and soiled, ragged underclothes." Perry's is a jocularity devoid of irony: there is no indirection, no doubleness, and Perry never undercuts his own imperturbable poise. That affable quality seems not really a function of a sensibility, and Perry makes no attempt to craft a "voice" or to project his own sense of self. Rather it is an aspect of the essay's, and Perry's, cultural situation.

The essay speaks with the authority of the *Saturday Evening Post*. For three decades, the *Saturday Evening Post*, having captured what looked like the center of American culture, held it, by gathering for its immense circulation a group of fictions and feature pieces, even illustrations and advertising copy, that implicitly defined what was interesting and pertinent, gratifying and essential, threatening and disturbing, charming and funny in contemporary life. It goes without saying that those norms were the norms of the middle and nothing about the magazine was ever expected to speak to the extremes, of wealth and poverty, or of politics, or of taste or education or cosmopolitan experience. Perry writes to that middlebrow, middle-class audience from well within its circle of assent.

Of the bipolar cluster of images that form the center of his essay, almost all of the qualities of Philadelphia that are good and true, pleasant and reassuring are either recalled from the historical past or are observed, in a diminished but charming way, as extensions of the past surviving in the present. What distresses Perry, on the other hand, what seems to him ugly, false, and threatening, is, almost exclusively, what he sees around him in the city of 1947. Alleys that still have hitching posts give him pleasure; so do genteel ladies at Wanamaker's Tea Room. Both have the requisite atavistic flavor. Philadelphia's drinking water, on the contrary, seems to him undrinkable, and its street maintenance defies travel. Independence Hall is alive and deeply moving; but City Hall is a "monstrosity." The Philadelphia of the past can be defined by the giants who walked its streets, from Franklin to Cyrus Curtis. And remnants of their works can still be seen. But the heroic dimension is absent from the corrupt and unimaginative city of 1947, and only two figures from the present, orchestral conductors, are mentioned at all. Without quite saying so, perhaps without meaning to, Perry has transformed a journalistic assessment of Philadelphia into a myth of decline.

Nothing in the present consoles Perry. The virtuosity of manufacturing in the postwar decade, some of it artful and skillful, is mentioned in a toneless series: "Stetson hats, Whitman's candies, Disston, Plumb and Yankee tools, Fels-Naptha soap." The breadth of its public arts, its jazz and its theater, for example, does not engage him: he mentions Philadelphia as a "try-out town for Broadway theater companies." Much that defines the city is apparently not worth remarking, the quality of its local journalism, for example. And no ordinary person then alive catches Perry's attention, no cabdriver or streetcar conductor, no waiter or clerk, no one who, in some representative moment, voices a fragment of the city's character. The mix of the city's Irish, Italian, and German neighborhoods, its pockets of East European and Asian ethnicity, both the vitality and the oppression of its very large black population—none of these makes an impression that Perry wishes to integrate into his essay.

It is not that Perry has it all wrong. I have argued that it is specious to "grade" earlier travelers on their fidelity or their perspicacity. There was corruption and complacency enough in the Philadelphia of the forties to justify every despairing word. And of course he is not alone in finding that the most attractive aspects of Philadelphia are those that carry a sense of the past. That he did not know where to look to find what energy and color and diversity the city did have to offer was a consequence of his audience, his magazine, and his own middlebrow location. In place of the actual city of 1947, whatever that would be, Perry imagines the city as the embodiment of a golden age undermined by 150 years of dry rot.

It is a pleasant enough essay to read but difficult to admire now: its range is narrow, its ethos smug, and the grace of its style covers a not very expansive spirit. But we cannot recover the response that the essay would have evoked in 1947 because we have lived with a hundred versions of the essay in the half-century since—meditations, laments, on the decline of cities in general, Philadelphia in particular, by writers both clever and leaden, right, left, and center, melancholy observations on the flight to the suburbs and the loss of an innocent, golden age of urban life. Perry's essay stands at the beginning of that fifty-year tradition of urban elegy; we stand at the end. And thus his essay is less derivative of other people's work than it is likely to seem to us; it is more original and probably far more difficult for him to have written than it may seem, now, to have been. Granting the essay the plausibility of its time and place, it begins to come back into focus in a somewhat different way. It is an imagination of Philadelphia. As a report of the life of the city, it is badly flawed, but as a vision of the city, it is whole and self-consistent.

Gathering the impressions of Philadelphia by people who do not live there, I decided to limit the data to writing since 1800. It is an arbitrary date, of course. But visiting the city in the eighteenth century was a different experience from visiting it in the two centuries since. William Birch published his great *City of Philadelphia* in 1800, the first attempt to capture pictorially the principal "views" of any American city and to

catch, as well, something of the city's élan. A number of the great institutions of the city were in place by the turn of the century. And the city
was large enough, complex and subtle enough by 1800 that visiting it
had become a rich and dense experience in a way in which it had not
been. Benjamin Franklin's arrival in Philadelphia is a touching and
powerful moment in American autobiography and American myth. But
it seems artificial to connect his sense of the city in 1723 (or for that
matter the gathering of the members of the Continental Congress fifty
years after) with the city that greeted travelers in the nineteenth and
twentieth centuries.

There is, to be sure, an infinity of responses to Philadelphia—some
unspoken, some inscribed on a postcard or lost in a diary. Even as I
write this sentence, although it is five miles from my desk and I cannot
see it, I know that a tour bus is parking in front of Independence Hall.
An hour ago it left the New Jersey Turnpike, has crossed the Delaware
River, and has traveled for ten minutes into the city; and fifty passengers,
at this moment, are alighting and beginning to compose fifty personal
versions of Penn's great city. It is, however, the impressions of writers
that I gather here, people who have written down what they have seen
with sufficient style and wit so that someone published what they wrote
and someone else elected to keep it on a shelf.

Gather together a few impressions of anything and they begin to fall
into patterns, of course. Responses to cities are likely to be especially
patterned. The attractions of cities, after all, are well publicized; certain
features of the tone and temper of most cities are potential subject matter
for small talk, even by people who have never been there; and much
travel writing is intensely intertextual, each writer describing a particular place by drawing as much upon other writers' impressions as upon
direct observation. As I have already suggested, however, responses to
Philadelphia are often unpredictable and the patterns into which they
fall are not at all what one might expect.

I have tried to let those patterns declare themselves. They have often
surprised me. But in half a lifetime of living in it, Philadelphia has often
seemed to me mysterious, even inscrutable. And so it has given me pleasure to find that the city has inscribed itself on the imaginations of two
centuries of visitors in ways that are often compelling but unpredictable,
a parallel city to the place on the map and the street under foot, a city of
the mind, an imagined Philadelphia.

1

Mastering Philadelphia

Cities are incomprehensible. They baffle the intelligence of even the most resolute experience: too big, too diverse, too secret. Part of what a Hugo or a Balzac novel is "about" is the only partly successful assault on the intelligibility of Paris. Dickens gives us something approaching the whole of London, knowing all the while how odd his angle of vision is and how fragmentary his report. Joyce's Dublin is caught and rendered with an astounding multiplicity and fidelity; but surely part of the effect of *Ulysses* is the sustained appearance of disintegration that leaves the reader unable to find something that feels like the whole of Dublin. Responding to this element of inscrutability, writers for two centuries have reached for a metaphor (or a symbolic, highly charged, descriptive mode) that not only points to that inscrutability but suggests as well the unease that accompanies it. To say that a city is a maze, for example, is to suggest that it is spatially complex in a way that frustrates a rational approach to its understanding; and it suggests that there is about the city a quality rather like a malicious game, with the experiencing self an unwilling victim. Or, to render the city as insufficient in its direction signs, confusing in its pattern, and full of a sullen and hostile populace for whom the merest request for direction is seen as offensive—all of this accomplishes the same purpose, which is to define the nature of urban experience as being inimical to individual consciousness.

Imagine a continuity with Gogol at its beginning. Here, for example, is a quintessentially characteristic Gogolian moment, from "The Overcoat." Akaky Akakievich is in an unfamiliar part of St. Petersburg; it is night, the streets are ill-lit, and the houses seem featureless and indistinguishable. "In the distance, God knows where, a light glimmered in a watchman's hut which seemed to be standing on the very edge of the world."[1] It is a moment before the devastating theft of Akaky's overcoat;

but there is nothing special about that moment's dull, vague sense of menace: St. Petersburg is always oddly lit in Gogol and the streets are always intimidating. At the nearer end of the continuum, consider a haunting but lesser-known story by Saul Bellow called "Looking for Mr. Green." The central character, who is white, attempts to deliver welfare checks in a black district of Chicago, particularly a check to someone named Green. "So he started again. He had four dark blocks to go, past open lots, condemned houses, old foundations, closed schools, black churches, mounds. . . ."[2] He muses on the waves of people who have moved through those streets, inscribing the area with their traces yet leaving it devoid of meaning. And the story concludes without his having found Mr. Green. Between those reference points lie countless comparable examples of the city as labyrinth and nightmare, resistant, hostile, and beyond comprehension.

Perhaps the locus classicus for a theory of the relation of city to self is Simmel's magisterial essay "The Metropolis and Mental Life." Rationalized and "objective," connected to others by bonds of precisely measured money and time, metropolitan man, Simmel argues, insulates himself from the disorientations of the intensified nervous stimulation of life in the city.[3] Catching the diminished and anomic self of modern urban man, Simmel's description misses, all the same, the haunted, dreamlike quality evoked by Gogol, Bellow, and a multitude of writers between–Hawthorne, Poe, and Melville, for example.[4] Kafka, to be sure, defines such an experience for the modern period, and his influence is everywhere. But the dream city, oppressive and inscrutable, has been a fixture of the American imagination for two hundred years.

In contrast to that general sense of the city in the inner life of American experience, the responses to Philadelphia by those who do not already live there are startling and extraordinary. People encountering Philadelphia for the first time do not think it is a maze or a vortex. House numbers can be found; streets meet other streets, by and large, at right angles; and any fool can tell you the directions to where you want to go. Visitors do not think Philadelphia is dimly lit or shrouded in a mist. It is crisp and clear. Visitors sometimes, in fact, remark on the clarity of the light, as if the absence of tall buildings and the consequent absence of pervasive shadow leave the city in a kind of lovely nakedness. They do not think the city two-leveled–a public self and a dark, hidden, secret self. Visitors sometimes remark on the reserve of the citizens, their guarded, private quality. But visitors generally think of that quality as being a perfectly wholesome, if puzzling, trait. It is not as if there were large areas of the city that were thought to be demimonde, or embarrassing, or inaccessible to the nonnative.

Scottish soldier, novelist, journalist, and traveler Thomas Hamilton approached the city from the Delaware River, as travelers generally did in the 1840s, finding "nothing striking" in his first view of Philadelphia.

Spires may be monsters in architecture, but they are beautiful monsters, and the eye feels a sad want of them as it wanders over the unvaried extent of dull uniform building presented by Philadelphia. When one enters the city the scene is certainly improved, but not much. The streets are rather respectable than handsome, but there is every where so much appearance of real comfort, that the traveller is at first delighted with this Quaker paradise. . . . The vehicle rolls on; he praises the cleanness and neatness of the houses, and every street that presents itself seems an exact copy of those which he has left behind. In short, before he has got through half the city, he feels an unusual tendency to relaxation about the region of the mouth, which ultimately terminates in a silent but prolonged yawn.[5]

For the moment, what is important is not so much the substance of Hamilton's observations as their rhythm. Within the space of a single paragraph, seemingly within a very short period of time, he has moved from the interest of an approaching traveler to boredom. He has levered up what the city has to offer of complexity and intricacy. And he has discovered the city's secret, which is that it has no secret. Nearly all travelers remark on the lowness of the city's silhouette and the regularity of its plan. It is not surprising that they should do so. What is surprising is that they think they find the city so knowable, so lacking in mystery and depth.

Lady Hardy, an English traveler later in the century, approaches Philadelphia with an almost naive tone of wonder and admiration, never undercut by anything resembling the sardonic condescension of Hamilton. The city shines in the sun; unlike Hamilton, she finds no lack of spires and domes; the streets are broad, busy, and festive; the buildings are magnificent—"marble fronts, marble columns, marble steps, marble everywhere." Mr. Lippincott, she reports, has published a guide to the city, which the thoughtful visitor would do well to keep so that "when you have 'done' the city, you will not throw aside your guide, but keep it as a pleasant refresher to your memory in after days."

Sedate and orderly, severe and self-possessed, the city has an old-world quality to it.

There are no overcrowded quarters here, no narrow courts or gloomy alleys, no tall tenement houses, like rabbit warrens, swarming with human creatures, sheltering hundreds within its reeking, dilapidated walls, where there is scarcely room for a score to live and breathe in. . . . No grim poverty parades the streets, no sickly faces turn to the wall, no wolf-eyed hunger lurks in corners. . . . Every man, from the lowest rung in the ladder, can rear his family in a home of his own if he pleases; rent is cheap, and the smallest cottage has its bath-room, wash-house, and patch of garden ground.[6]

Writing more than thirty-five years after Hamilton, it is a somewhat altered Philadelphia that Lady Hardy responds to. Obviously she has nothing in common with Hamilton in matters of taste and sensibility, judgment and personal style. What they do share is the ease with which they think they have grasped the essence of Philadelphia, a common self-satisfaction in having exhausted its possibilities. During the years between Hamilton's and Lady Hardy's visits, the population of the city (and the immediately surrounding area in the years before incorporation) had grown from more than three hundred thousand to more than eight hundred thousand. Yet both tourists respond to the city as if they were visiting a snug and homogeneous city of a tenth its size.

Midway between the journeys of Hamilton and Hardy, an English clergyman named James Dixon published his *Personal Narrative of a Tour through a Part of the United States and Canada*, an expression of his "desire to make the Methodist body in England acquainted with the state and progress of their system of religion in the United States." Although he never loses sight of his purpose for very long, the state of Methodism often becomes secondary to the pleasures of travel for its own sake: the book is ingenious in its observations, sometimes lyric in its writing, and extraordinarily extensive in its travels. But the experience of Philadelphia occupies less than two pages of text. Dixon approaches from the Delaware River and is struck by the perfection of the setting, which seems to him suggestive of Paradise. But once into the city he is obsessed with the regularity of the plan and the uniformity of the buildings. It is the prim Quaker mentality, he thinks, that has molded the physical features of the city. Alas, "Time would not allow us to remain long. I had only an opportunity of running into one or two public buildings; of passing down a few streets, so as to obtain a general idea of the place; of getting a hasty dinner, and then starting off towards Baltimore."[7] Again, the tone and the sensibility are different but the closure is the same. The traveler, after what seems about an hour in the city, has understood it, in some sense sufficient to himself exhausted it. And he is ready to leave.

What does not appear in any of the three accounts is the quarter of the population in midcentury that was foreign born and the various waves of hostility toward them by the native-born; a virulent race problem; a large indigent population; a totally inadequate law enforcement system; the constant threat of epidemic. George Lippard, a Philadelphia journalist, published his novel *The Quaker City* in 1844. It was hugely successful both in the United States and abroad. Published slightly after Hamilton's tour, it describes conditions that Hamilton could have seen for himself. Once published, it would have been known to nearly any literate reader for the rest of the nineteenth century. At its beginning, Lippard constructs a scenario portraying a dying lawyer who charges Lippard, in the preface to the novel, to tell the truth about Philadelphia, which "is not so pure as it looks." "The city which William Penn built upon hope and honor,–whose root was planted deep in the soil of truth and peace" has become a place of "poison and rottenness, Riot, Arson, Murder and Wrong."[8]

Whether one had read Lippard or not, the city's dark problems, by the 1840s, had reached a level of obviousness that could be ignored only by a strange and evasive act of the mind. But long before the publication of *The Quaker City*, the complexity of the city was surely apparent. One of the most desperately stricken areas was a mere five blocks from Independence Hall. A traveler looking for crowded housing could have found some: through the latter half of the nineteenth century, the average number of occupants for a single dwelling was between six and seven. And a curious visitor looking for houses without marble steps would not have had far to look.[9]

Not all travelers, it is true, took so narrowly circumscribed a tour of official, intelligible Philadelphia, clean, proper, and nonthreatening. Tocqueville, for one, took an ominous view of the city's underclass. The United States, he writes, has two very large cities, New York and Philadelphia. Both have large populations of the "lower ranks," which "constitute a rabble" of menacing proportions.

They consist of freed blacks . . . who are condemned by the laws and by public opinion to a hereditary state of misery and degradation. They also contain a multitude of Europeans who have been driven to the shores of the New World by their misfortunes or their misconduct.

Without civil rights, moved only by self-interest, such an underclass represented a threat to civil order which could only be restrained by a substantial armed force.[10]

William Chambers, the English encyclopedist, visiting in midcentury, recorded a much broader, multileveled Philadelphia than the standard tourist's view, not because he, like Tocqueville, shared an interest in *civitas* and its fragility, but rather because of his wonderfully lively, animated curiosity about the city. Speech accents obviously intrigue him, as do dress and manners, the vitality of street life, the tendency of Philadelphians to heat the interior of their homes to an insufferable degree, retail sales, an umbrella factory, the importation of coal, the mint, the penitentiary, the publishing industry.[11] Tocqueville in one way, Chambers in another, demonstrate that it was by no means inevitable that a nineteenth-century visitor to Philadelphia would record observations that were facile, reductive, apparently honorific but ultimately condescending. Still, there they are, all of those high-speed visitors, eager to remark on the straight streets and hit the high road for Baltimore. Some of the reasons for that mode of response to the city are immediately obvious; some are not.

One thing that is clear is that the three travelers (and nearly all visitors to Philadelphia in the nineteenth and twentieth centuries) did not set out, explicitly and deliberately, to visit Philadelphia. Such a visit was either one part of a plan to visit much larger areas of the United States or it was a place to pass through on the way to somewhere else. Philadelphia was not then, and has not been since, a major destination. There has never been much desire in the anticipation of it. A nineteenth-century traveler would desire Niagara Falls or Saratoga; a twentieth-century traveler desires Fifth Avenue, perhaps, or the Golden Gate Bridge. But places in Philadelphia are words in the mind, not longings of the heart.

It also becomes immediately obvious, reading those earlier travelers, that the single concept that most clearly governs their anticipation of Philadelphia is the idea of Quakerism. Variations of the word "Quaker" appear, centrally and obsessively, in the imagination of the city. But it is Quaker style more than Quaker substance that occupies the visitor's mind. Travelers never come to the city hoping to visit a Quaker meeting or to understand Quaker ideas more fully. Least of all does anyone hope to meet a Quaker and have a conversation. Often, one senses a slight anxiety, as if the traveler is not entirely sure whether

Quakers still exist and whether he could be certain if he saw one. Still, despite the nearly total lack of interest in a real Quaker presence in Philadelphia, there is no American city (except, ultimately, Salt Lake City) in which a sectarian ethos is imagined to pervade its very temper and its rhythms. Insofar as travelers expect to find a muted, self-effacing urban scene, short on decoration and ostentation, long on wholesomeness and the virtues of consensus, then that is what they find – a Quakerized cityscape. Having imputed Quaker simplicity to the city before he arrives, the visitor finds – Quaker simplicity.

Part of the tension and the excitement of visiting an unfamiliar place lies in the perception and the degree of difference between the manners and the morals one discovers and the range of experience one already knows. The visitor, noting the local customs, tries to find the right way to respond to the otherness of the others. Supercilious amusement at that otherness suits the temperament of some travelers, compassionate curiosity others, and dispassionate analysis still others. But in whatever way, the traveler, seeing the unique features of landscape, people, speech, diet, whatever, tries to crack the code, read the signs, understand the particular ways of the new place as opposed to the familiar place. Reading those nineteenth-century travelers, it is striking how little they find to remark on that is different. Very few things seem surprising. There are the straight streets and the marble steps; there is an amazing abundance of municipal water. But until the appearance of City Hall at the end of the nineteenth century, public buildings in Philadelphia look to visitors pretty much like public buildings somewhere else. Some of the streets, travelers discover, are named for trees, some are merely given numbers. Occasionally a visitor will remark on the weather, which is either too hot or just right. Occasionally a visitor will remark on the beauty of Philadelphia women. It is all, in most accounts, rather distant and uninvolving, as if seen through the wrong end of a telescope. When the distance collapses and a traveler seems to draw close and pay attention – Mrs. Trollope, among others, recoils at chewing tobacco, for example, and Dickens really listens to the patterns of speech – it is refreshing precisely because the traveler is seeing differences.

Mere differences from one place to another are, of course, not necessarily very interesting. Differences are most interesting to the traveler, and the reader, insofar as they produce unease. Impenetrable idioms and an unfamiliar cuisine, for example, leave the traveler off balance, anxious, and uncomfortable; and it is such temporary instability that invites the reader into the drama of the narrative. Ultimately, by the end of the nineteenth century, what strikes visitors who are sensitive to it is the corruption of the city, its magnitude and audacity. Otherwise, there is little in the visitors' accounts that suggests that very much in the experience of the city seems odd, or eccentric, or threatening, or destabilizing, or shocking, or local in some guarded and parochial way that resists interpretation by a nonnative.

One reason that the city seems so muted, so nondramatic, so lacking in differentness to so many writers is that most travelers in the nineteenth century approached from the north, having just spent a period of time in New York and, traveling through New Jersey, arrived at the port of Philadelphia, busy enough but undramatic, the recollection of New York still fresh in the mind. Even now, when travel routes are various and flexible, it is not unusual for a traveler to arrive in Philadelphia with a sense of New York pervading his consciousness of American urban life. Defined, for two centuries, by its energy, its multiplicity, its aggressiveness, and its centrality in American cultural life, New York has been everything that Philadelphia was not. Philadelphia, consequently, could be seen as gentle and comfortable on the one hand or bland and uncomplicated on the other, the traveler being not particularly aware that he had carried with him a set of norms derived from the incomparable New York.

From a different point of view, consider the social density of the city through the eyes of the travelers. One notices that Hamilton, Hardy, and Dixon all describe the geography of Philadelphia but say little about people, visible people, pedestrians, street vendors perhaps, official figures such as policemen, the unavoidable poor. The city, for them, seems to exist without noise. Sometimes, reading the travelers, such an absence looks like a gap, a hole, a dimension of experience really there but not noticed and not recorded. Sometimes it seems as if there really *isn't* anybody on the streets. The subject of countless jokes in the early twentieth century ("I went to Philadelphia but it was closed"), the comparative absence of street life is best recorded in 1838 by Captain Marryat, who writes not as if he were echoing other people's stale jokes but as if the observation were original with him.

The first idea which strikes you when you arrive at Philadelphia is that it is Sunday: everything is so quiet, and there are so few people stirring; but by the time that you have paraded half a dozen streets, you come to a conclusion that it must be Saturday, as that day is, generally speaking, a washing-day.

The city is so liberally supplied with water from the Schuylkill waterworks that the citizens seem continually to be washing—marble steps, doors, windows, and pavements. Marryat soon drops the conceit and moves on to other areas of observation. But he has left the impression, in its ur form: arriving in Philadelphia, it is either Sunday or it looks as if it is.[12]

Only in recent years have we begun to understand the basis for our varying impressions of streets and people, as the result of the kinds of urban analysis done by Jane Jacobs, William H. Whyte, Kevin Lynch, and Tony Hiss or the work of such microsociologists as Erving Goffman. Consider Goffman's brilliant essay "Normal Appearances," in his *Relations in Public*, in which he describes areas of vulnerability in public life against a background of perceived normality. One's "furnished frame," as one moves through ordinary experience, consists of an ever-changing enclosure of walls, floors, ceilings, doors, furniture, mailboxes, parked cars. One assumes the elements of the frame to be neutral, realizing, however, that the wall might contain a hidden microphone, the parked car a bomb. In an ingenious coinage, Goffman writes of "lurk lines," by which he means not only the area behind one's back but areas hidden from view: "the area behind doors when these are open; inside unlocked closets, and around sharp bends in passageways; the floor of a car's back seat for those who enter the front door; the small space between individuals who are tightly packed." Goffman plays back and forth between the permutations of alarm, the signs that warn of vulnerability, and, on the other hand, the various signals of assurance, routine, and security.[13]

Imagine a trip by a traveler to nineteenth-century Philadelphia. There would have been excursions, perhaps, to Girard College and Eastern State Penitentiary, to the waterworks and adjacent areas of Fairmount Park. But by and large, the visit would have taken place within a very circumscribed area of the central city. Whoever the traveler's host might have been, there would have been vast areas of the city where he, the host, would not ordinarily have gone for his own purposes, certainly would never have taken a guest, and perhaps would never have been for any reason. Elizabeth Robins Pennell, the wife of the illustrator, writes in 1914 of that tight little area in a tone at once bemused and accepting.

On the map Philadelphia might stretch over a vast area with the possibility of spreading indefinitely, but for social purposes it was shut in to the East and West by the Delaware and Schuylkill, to the North and the South by a single line of the old rhyming line of the streets: "Chestnut, Walnut, Spruce and Pine." I have not the antiquarian knowledge to say who drew that rigid line. . . . I have heard the line ridiculed but never explained. No geographical boundary has been, or could be, more arbitrary, but there it was, there it is, and the Philadelphian who crosses it risks his good name. Nor can the stranger, though unwarned, disregard it with impunity.[14]

That amazingly circumscribed area would indeed have been a portion of Penn's original plan, a grid pattern; and the traveler, starting to walk down a block, would have been able to see the end of the block, where an intersecting street would cross it at right angles. The housing stock would, indeed, be uniform, and the commercial buildings would be rather similar to each other. The houses would abut the sidewalk, with no intervening space or vegetation (although, despite the absence of front yards, the city has always found ways of encouraging shade trees). Seeming to hide nothing, doors, probably four or five stone steps above the street level, would invite immediate access. Those central Philadelphia streets would, in other words, have offered a cityscape virtually devoid of "lurk lines," dark corners of mystery and menace, problematic turns and forks in the road. Of course Philadelphia has always had as many alleys, cul-de-sacs, and dark places as any old city. And visitors in more recent years have sometimes sought out the "little streets" as presenting a kind of atavistic charm. But it is the broad, bright, nonproblematic streets that appear in the visitors' accounts.

Just as obviously, anyone venturing into many of the areas a short distance from the center of the city would have found alarm and potential menace, not only quite plausibly there, among the unsavory citizens, but in the very shape of the environment, full of hiding places and threat. Only recently has the social history of the city begun to recover a sense of how dirty and dangerous a place much of the city really was.[15] But visitors did not go to those areas; there was nothing there that they came to see. If travelers found the city nonthreatening, not very complicated, and easily understood, it was, to some extent, because the style of those city streets that they happened to walk seemed to have nothing to hide, seemed to offer no haven for malevolence, each block an unbroken facade of normality, geometry, and conscious intent.

The grid pattern, not entirely original with Penn, seemed to define

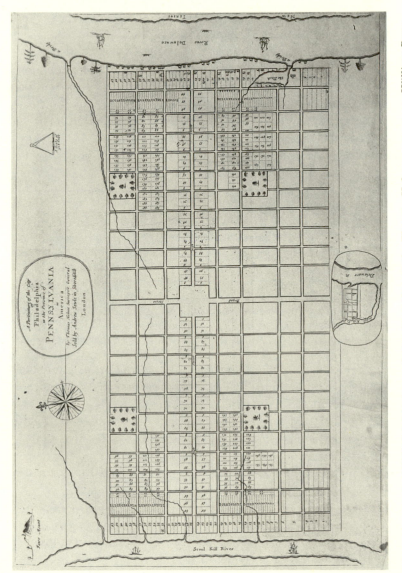

Figure 1. A map of Philadelphia drawn *before* its settlement by Thomas Holme, surveyor to William Penn (published in London in 1683), showing how essential all of its straight streets and right angles were to the idea of the city. Courtesy of the Library Company of Philadelphia.

a rationale of urban design so compelling that innumerable American cities adopted the model. The pervasiveness of the grid pattern has occasioned a range of responses, mostly negative, by such historians of the city as Lewis Mumford, John W. Reps, and Sam Bass Warner, the allegation being, in one form or another, that straight streets and regular blocks do not serve complex human needs.[16]

It is a charge that Kevin Lynch answers, not casually but on the basis of a substantial body of research into what Lynch calls the "legibility" of a city, the ease with which its citizens can recognize its parts and relate them to a coherent whole. To put it one way, insofar as a city is legible, its inhabitants tend always to know where they are, never to be lost. The key skeletal elements of a city's pattern tend to be internalized, in a rhythmic and sensuous way; and the clarity of their direction is an essential aspect of that internal coherence.

> The line of motion should have clarity of direction. The human computer is disturbed by long successions of turnings, or by gradual, ambiguous curves which in the end produce major directional shifts. The continuous twistings of Venetian calli or of the streets in one of Olmstead's romantic plans, or the gradual turning of Boston's Atlantic Avenue, soon confuse all but the most adaptive observers. . . . Observers seem to endow a path with a sense of pointing or irreversible direction, and to identify a street with the destination toward which it goes. A street is perceived, in fact, as a thing which goes toward something.[17]

One hardly needs to grant that Lynch has the better of the argument to conclude that his description of the legibility of cities bears precisely on the reaction of visitors to Philadelphia. The plan of the city is easily internalized into a mental map and the streets are intelligible and non-problematic for all of those nineteenth-century visitors because that is what people do, then and now, with a grid-shaped city.

It is not only its intelligible grid – its short blocks, its corners – but its continued coherence through the decades that draws the praise of William H. Whyte. The development of the city has clustered within the original conception of its plan, in an area two miles square, between the two rivers. "The center is precisely where it was planned to be. . . . One thing about Philadelphia: you know where you are."[18] Still, one recalls that legibility and coherence are capable of being read as monotony, an experience holding no mystery and inviting no penetration.

"At Philadelphia, 'the city of Brotherly Love,'" begins Charles Joseph Latrobe in 1835, "you are struck with the regularity of the streets, –

Figure 2. Chestnut Street in the 1840s, in a lithograph by Duval, draws the viewer into its perspective. The space of the street is broad, light, straight, and nonproblematic until it reaches the Delaware River. Courtesy of the Library Company of Philadelphia.

their numberless handsome mansions,–the lavish use of white and grey marble,–pleasant avenues and squares,–noble public institutions,–markets. . . ." Reading the sentence now, one feels the rhythm, the glazed eye, the inability to draw close and enter the life of the city, knowing that in short order Latrobe will have seen enough. In another sentence, he has. And it is on to Baltimore.[19]

Somewhere near the opposite extreme are those visitors who are clearly so fascinated with the intelligibility of the grid system that they are compelled to describe it with a numbing particularity. Anthony Trollope is among them. Visiting the city in the sixties, he begins his account with a few broad strokes and then describes the major streets, the intersecting streets, and the numbering of houses.

In the long streets the number of the houses are not consecutive, but follow the numbers of the cross-streets; so that a person living in Chestnut Street between

Tenth Street and Eleventh Street, and ten doors from Tenth Street, would live at
No. 1010. The opposite house would be No. 1011. It thus follows that the number
of the house indicates the exact block of houses in which it is situated.

He does not like the right-angle streets, Trollope adds, but he does find
it infinitely easier to find his way around in Philadelphia than he did in
New York.[20] The anonymous author of *Baggage and Boots; or Smith's
First Peep at America*, touring two decades later, begins to sound as if he
has been reading Trollope; it seems more likely, however, that he is fascinated by the city's grid in his own way. "Thus, the numbers of all the
houses in any street between the river and the first street are under 100,
between that and 2nd Street between 100 and 200. As soon as that is
crossed, the numbering commences at 201, 202. . . ."[21]

Both the glazed boredom of Latrobe and the obsessive fascination of
Trollope become less plausible responses to Philadelphia's grid as the
nineteenth century ends. The most obvious reason that those facile responses to the city begin to diminish is that the urban grid becomes so
widely adopted, in so many different places, that it would take an especially naive observer, or an especially Eurocentric one, to continue to
express amazement that streets in Philadelphia meet other streets at
regular intervals and at right angles. The other obvious reason is that,
by the end of the nineteenth century, the city had become so diverse and
so complex that to approach it expecting a "Quaker paradise" and finding it to be so when one arrived required a fixity of mind of extraordinary proportions.

In 1903, Lincoln Steffens, writing in *McClure's*, titled his muckraking essay "Philadelphia: Corrupt and Contented." It is one of the most
durable phrases, and concepts, ever attached to the city. It not only tem-
pers the sense of Philadelphia for many visitors for the rest of the century, or at least until a vigorous reform movement transformed city
government in the fifties. It represents a sensibility fascinated by hidden
layers of power and influence and money, a cast of mind only rarely
present in travelers of the nineteenth century. Philadelphia, in Steffens's
view of it, is still far from a maze or a vortex. With some industry, its
mysteries can be levered up, its entrapments avoided. But it is not all
surface either, to be understood in an afternoon.

A few years earlier, Walt Whitman had made one of his customary
trips across the river from Camden. It was early spring and "it was good
to be on Chestnut street."

The peddlers on the sidewalk – ('sleeve-buttons, three for five cents") – the hand-some little fellow with canary-bird whistles – the cane men, toy men, toothpick men – the old woman squatted in a heap on the cold stone flags, with her basket of matches, pins and tape – the young negro mother, sitting, begging, with her two little coffee-color'd twins on her lap – the beauty of the cramm'd conserva-tory of rare flowers, flaunting reds, yellows, snowy lilies, incredible orchids, at the Baldwin mansion near Twelfth street – the show of fine poultry, beef, fish, at the restaurants – the china stores, with glass and statuettes....[22]

The passage is little short of astonishing, after a century of visitors' ac-counts in which nothing much seems to be bought or sold, no one worth noting or celebrating or particularizing seems to be on the street. It is like Mayhew's Victorian London, like turn-of-century photographs of lower Manhattan, diverse and lovingly observed, celebrated.

Henry James, returning to the United States in 1906 after years of living abroad, found he could have it both ways, although it was by no means easy to do so. In his essay on Philadelphia in *The American Scene*, he records the impression that the city was complex and elusive; at the same time, he records the impression that the city was simple and ob-vious. It is a masterful essay, devious, dense, and ironic.[23]

Reaching for a sense of the city's style, he self-consciously gropes for a word. By and by, the word appears. "Philadelphia, incontestably then, was the American city of the large type that didn't *bristle*." He likes the literal feel of the word. Philadelphia's quills do not stand erect: it is, precisely, a flat city. And he likes the metaphorical resonance: it is not a city of great emotional pressure, of great energy and élan, "neither eager, nor grasping, nor pushing." Simple enough. It sounds like an ele-gant variation of the old observation that Philadelphia is a dull and mo-notonous place. Yet "Philadelphia, manifestly, was beyond any other American city, a *society*," as, for example, New York, which bristled, was not, and least of all Chicago, which supremely bristled, could not have been imagined to be. In other words, a corollary of the apparent sim-plicity of Philadelphia is – its complexity.

The rhetoric of depth runs through James's essay: one perceives and guesses, courts intimacy, studies and observes, one penetrates, or tries to, one's subject withholds, one tries "to 'read' into" the American scene "as much as he reads out." Partly, what engages James's feeling of the layered, complex reality of Philadelphia is its visible sense of the past, its haunting, tangible evidence of its own history. Mostly, however, it is a larger, pervasive sense of the city's duality that engages James. He

reads the city with all of the precious, elite aestheticism of the most sheltered and self-satisfied nineteenth-century tourist. At the same time, he
reads its underside with the fierceness of a Lincoln Steffens.

The place . . . was two distinct things–a Society, from far back, the society I had
divined, the most genial and delightful one could think of, and then, parallel to
this, and not within it, nor quite altogether above it, but beside it and beneath it,
behind it and before it, enclosing it as in a frame of fire in which it still had the
secret of keeping cool, a proportionate City, the most incredible that ever was,
organized all for plunder and rapine, the gross satisfaction of official appetite,
organized for eternal iniquity and impunity.

It is the quintessential American case in which "sane Society and pesti-
lent City . . . successfully cohabit." Adding an astonishingly apocalyptic
image that sounds less as if it comes from 1906 than from some year
considerably closer to our own time, James remarks that society in Philadelphia dances as gallantly as it does because it dances, "all consciously, on the thin crust of a volcano."[24]

All cities, of course, are beyond describing–too large, too complex,
too contradictory. For all that, some cities lend themselves to a kind of
writing that seems, at its best, authentic and not reductive. Strikingly
original observations do get made about Philadelphia and James's essay
is one of them. But, more than with any other major American city, a
large amount of the writing about it occupies a remarkably narrow band
of mind, and affect, and language.

In the fifties, Camus traveled in the United States. Passing through
Philadelphia, he recorded a single sentence in his journals: "In Philadelphia, enormous gas tanks tower over little cemeteries full of flowers."[25] It is probably a synthetic image but one knows what he is after:
the ironic juxtaposition of the sweet and sentimental ethnic cemeteries
of South Philadelphia with the vast oil refineries not far away. It is epiphanic and striking and probably original. What is not original about it
Camus could not have known and that is its rhythm. Having captured
the essence of the city in a single image, he moves on, as if his curiosity
about the city were exhausted, his interest in it dispelled. There is something about the city and visitors, their expectations and their experience, that have induced a multitude of others before him to think too
quickly that they have understood the city.

2

Walking Philadelphia

Well over thirty years after its publication, Jane Jacobs's *The Death and Life of Great American Cities* is still arresting in its argument, humane in its rhetoric.[1] It is hard to know whether she single-handedly altered the way we look at cities or whether she spoke most eloquently for a trend that might have happened without her. But one reads in her early pages of the received wisdom of urban valuation at the time she wrote–the work of Lewis Mumford and Le Corbusier, and others less well known but equally decisive in the field–and one realizes how dated, abstract, and inhumane the "Radiant Garden Cities" of those earlier urban planners seem now and how vital her ideas continue to be. Mumford and Le Corbusier, Clarence Stein, Catherine Bauer, and Sir Raymond Unwin, Jacobs's counterexamples, all wrote out of a discontent with cities and a wish to turn them into something else. Jacobs wrote out of love for the sustaining, energizing mixture of uses to which cities are put, their diversity and clutter. People who have read her book see cities differently from the way they might have before she wrote it. And a multitude of people who have not read her book see cities differently as a result of a shift in attention and valuation that she did much to encourage.

Partly, Jacobs's new approach was methodological–a distrust of generalizations and a wish to let her conclusions emerge only from an inductive observation of the daily, intimate experience of cities. Partly, it was temperamental–the polemic of a willed amateur, a witness, opposing the cool abstractions of the professionals. Partly it was situational–a book not about planning but about being there. Concerned with many aspects of urban vitality, Jacobs's book is, for all of its breadth of vision, nonetheless, in some irreducible sense, a book about walking in cities.

William H. Whyte's incomparable *City: Rediscovering the Center* participates in that altered valuation of urban space. Whyte answers

questions of urban use not from his armchair but from the results of
fixed, hidden cameras, aimed at the streets themselves, from which he
assembled systematic observations of the way people move, and how
fast, and how they avoid bumping into each other, and whether they ever
sit, and where and how they converse, and whether they eat, and whether
the sunlight ever reaches them, and, most important, whether they show
signs of enjoying life. More of his observations are drawn from New York
than from any other city; as one would expect, it is cities with a vibrant
center that most engage him—Tokyo, Copenhagen, San Francisco. Now
and then, he is struck with the opposite, an urban situation that defeats an
encounter with the street. "At Houston Center," he writes, "you can drive
in from the freeway to the garage, walk through a skyway to one tower,
thence to another, work, shop, lunch, work, and then head back to the
freeway without ever having set foot in Houston at all." [2]

Like Whyte's, Jane Jacobs's observations come more from New York
than elsewhere. However she, like Whyte, also likes certain areas of
Philadelphia, likes them so much that they form central exhibits in her
argument. Of the original squares in Penn's city plan, two are exemplary
in opposite ways. Washington Square is unappealing and sometimes
sinister because the nearby properties are largely office buildings, providing a narrow range of use for the park. It is as uncongenial as it is
because not enough people walk there. Rittenhouse Square is Jacobs's
shining example of urban space well used, because people do walk
there, for a multitude of purposes, at all hours of the day and night, with
an obvious sense of security, well-being, and pleasure in being there.
For both Jacobs and Whyte, the irreducible unit of urban life is one person, on foot, among a society of others who share the street. And Philadelphia, for both of them, offers an attractive example from time to time
because it is, demonstrably, a city in which people really do walk.

Jacobs and Whyte have foregrounded the life of the streets, induced
us to attend to it, both by the incisiveness of their writing and by their
insistence on what we have gradually come to realize independently,
that there is a large and growing number of cities in which people do
not walk. Looking back from the perspective of Jacobs, Whyte, and the
considerable number of urbanologists writing now who share a rich re-
sponsiveness to the essential experience of walking, one realizes how
persistent that dimension of the life of the city is in travelers' accounts of
visits to Philadelphia. Again and again, visitors explicitly write about
walking in the city. Benjamin Franklin, newly arrived from Boston, walk-

ing up Market Street from the wharf one cold day in October 1723 with a loaf of bread under his arm, was not the first person to experience the streets of Philadelphia in a way so vivid as to remember it years later and write it down, and he was very far from being the last.

The fact that many impressions of Philadelphia are more brief than full, more perfunctory than copious with the details of the city, more distant than involved would seem irreconcilable with the role of Philadelphia as one of the great walking cities of North America. The two dimensions *are* paradoxical; a stable irony, they do not cancel each other out. And perhaps the best response to that odd coexistence of apparently contrasting traits is to say that they are by no means the only paradox that attaches to the city. Even travelers who seem to have found little in the city to detain them seem drawn to the experience of walking its streets in a way that is very far from the case with most other cities.

The Scottish traveler Lieutenant Colonel A. M. Maxwell charmingly titled his travel narrative *A Run through the United States during the Autumn of 1840*. However colloquial and metaphorical his phrase "run through," there is, everywhere in his response to Philadelphia, a sense of foot meeting pavement with the leisured rhythm of a lover of the streets, not the kind of airy view of the sights that travel accounts so often suggest, rather a concrete sense of physicality.

We have been strolling this evening through the really splendid city of Philadelphia. It is built on the right bank of the Delaware, and not far distant from the confluence of the Schuylkill with that river. There are many fine streets; Chestnut Street and High Street are magnificent; they are very wide, long, and perfectly straight and level.[3]

The width of the city is, he reports, two miles, and the vigor of his diction makes it seem as if he has walked it; the streets are mostly "laid with blocks of wood instead of stone." The shops are "gaudy," the streets, when they are lighted, are "brilliant," the public buildings are tasteful, the women are beautiful, and, walking Chestnut Street, he is reminded of Milan. Ultimately he takes an omnibus to the Fairmount Waterworks, noting the view and the promenade, implicitly making clear that the waterworks is too far to walk or he would have walked there. His walking the city is not explicit and he does not discuss walking as a choice, among others, for moving about the city; still, the essential fact of his walking is consistently there, in the selection of verbs, the eye-level details, the sensuousness of his encounter with the city.

Figure 3. An etching from Robert Waln, Jr., *The Hermit in America*: Walking on Chestnut Street in 1819–stylized, fashionable, and above all social. Courtesy of the Library Company of Philadelphia.

Mrs. Trollope writes that she spends her mornings in Philadelphia asking the residents what must be seen. The rest of the day she spends seeking out "all that the answers told us it was necessary to see." Discovering the sights, she adds, is easier in Philadelphia than in any other city. "You have nothing to do but walk up one straight street, and down another, till all the parallelograms have been threaded."[4]

One thing that is common to both Lieutenant Colonel Maxwell's strolling the many fine streets and Mrs. Trollope's threading the parallelograms is the ease and intelligibility of the city, its "legibility," as I have described it, drawing upon Kevin Lynch. But there are many aspects of the city and its culture in the nineteenth century that contribute to the widely shared feeling that Philadelphia is a place in which one walks, that it is natural and comfortable and pleasant to do so. And the sweet reason of Penn's grid system is only one of those aspects.

Imagine arriving at a place that looks like any number of other places. Lacking a set of visual, stylistic traits that seem unique to it, such a place has no definition; one searches the name of the local bank or the masthead of the local newspaper to confirm where one is: the cityscape does not reveal it. Déjà vu or *jamais vu*, one cannot be sure whether one has been here before or whether one has never been here. It is an experience common in twentieth-century travel, of course, the McDonald's, the Holiday Inn, the Midas Muffler shop. But interchangeable Main Streets and business blocks devoid of style are hardly exclusive features of this century. Tocqueville noted that places in America, even those with widely differing economies and topographies, tend to look the same. The appearance of similarity to other places is a sufficient deterrent to any wish to enter into the life of a city.

Travelers generally form an impression of Philadelphia immediately, before they have really seen the particular features of the city. What they base their impressions on is a generalized sense of style, the look that instantly distinguishes Philadelphia from Boston, New York, and Baltimore. No traveler ever seriously says that Philadelphia looks like another place or imitates another place or is easily confused with another place. Some travelers like its style immediately, some loathe it. But that visceral liking or not liking is based upon a very quick but totally convincing impression of the defining traits of the physical city of Philadelphia. Such a perception, of Philadelphia's own way of being a city, seems a precondition of a willingness to walk its streets.

The Hungarian intellectual Alexander Farkas de Bolon recorded his initial impressions of the city in 1831. Immediately obvious to the reader of his narrative now are those two features, a recognition of the uniqueness of the city's style and the compelling way in which the city beckons, so that the visitor wishes not only to see the sights but to walk.

> Many travellers write and say that Philadelphia is the most beautiful city in the world. I heard this exclusive praise also in Europe about so many towns that, although I expected Philadelphia to be beautiful, I did not imagine that after ten days' residence there, I should admit that the city is really one of the most lovely....
>
> First day we walked through the streets and inspected the most important parts of the city. The more parts we visited, the more my admiration increased.... I thought that I walked in the Athens or the Rome of the classic ages....[5]

Along with "legibility," Kevin Lynch adopts the word "imageability" to the inner response of an observer of a city's life. If his word "legibility" suggests that a city is a text, which can be read easily or not, "imageability" suggests that a city is a picture, which can be configured in the mind, seen in the consciousness, easily or not. A public image of a city,

Lynch explains, is "the overlap of many individual images" held more
or less in common by a substantial number of the people who live there.⁶
It is twentieth-century experience that Lynch is concerned with. But
travelers to a city have always tried to resolve it into a picture, perhaps
more precisely a coherent collage. And Farkas, in the passage above,
expresses such an attempt.

One of Lynch's case studies is Jersey City. If a resident is asked what
Jersey City "looks like," the respondent is baffled. Except for the view
of the New York skyline across the river, which is, of course, a picture of
another city, Jersey City doesn't look like anything. Its skyline is not
peculiar to Jersey City; neither its domestic nor its commercial architecture is in any way distinctive; there are no landmarks, nothing that
visually speaks to the uniqueness of Jersey City. One of Lynch's contrasting examples is Boston, which "looks like" many things, not only to
people from elsewhere who know some of the official views but also
to people who live there: the Charles River, Boston Common, Back Bay
houses, Fenway Park, Faneuil Hall, and Beacon Street. Although Lynch
does not discuss Philadelphia, it is surely "imageable" in the nineteenth century. It is Independence Hall and the Fairmount Waterworks,
straight streets with shade, narrow attached houses, red bricks, marble
steps, and shutters. Visitors know the look before they arrive: they could
not have escaped the engravings that sought to capture characteristic
scenes of Philadelphia style. Once here, they are happy to walk into the
streets where the visual motifs are repeated with an endlessly confirming rhythm.

The Irish actor Tyrone Power, traveling and acting in the 1830s,
makes the experience of visiting Philadelphia very much his own. But it
is striking how many of his perceptions are comparable to those of other
travelers in the decades of the mid-nineteenth century. The city occupies
a peninsula between two rivers and its streets run at right angles. The
north-south streets are numbered and the east-west streets are largely
named for trees. The housing is largely brick and the shutters are green.
The streets are broad, the pace is a little slow, and the tone is comfortable. All of this is to say that the city is "legible," in Lynch's word, (Power
says that the arrangement of the streets "renders the stranger's course
an exceeding easy one") and it is "imageable": within a day of arriving,
Power is beginning to assemble, from the evidence, a mental picture of
Philadelphia. Like all of the others, Power makes it abundantly clear
that he has gathered his impressions from walking and that he has

formed his conclusions about the residents from seeing them at eye level. He loves the market, which provides a kind of street theater, a variety of postures and dialects, especially the unassimilated Germanness of many of the street merchants, and he reproduces fragments of their dialect with an actor's zest. And several times he returns to the impression of the streets as being as inviting as they are because they are uncommonly clean, both the fronts of the houses, which he contrasts with the forbidding dinginess of British houses, and the pavement itself.[7]

Throughout the eighteenth century, commercial establishments in American cities had generally been houses, distinguished from residences by a sign. By the early nineteenth century, windows opening onto the street had begun to appear, so that businesses gradually took on the look of modern retail stores. A walk in central Philadelphia in the mid-nineteenth century such as those many travelers describe would have been partly devoted to what we now call window-shopping. It would not have been so a half-century before. Such a walk was also simultaneously an experience of the most memorable blocks of private housing since, throughout the nineteenth century and indeed up to the present time, Philadelphia retained a substantial residential core. And in addition, occurring within that mixture of commercial and residential buildings and not at all segregated from it were many of the more noteworthy public buildings. Travelers often shift their observations from the public to the private, the commercial to the residential, without much modulation or transition and little apparent surprise.

Surprised or not, there could have been few areas anywhere in the world that were at once so compact and so diverse. Diverse in its use, the area was diverse in the taste it ministered to: it was among the elegant retailers and the impressive architecture that Barnum established his museum in 1849, including copies of paintings from the Louvre and such "transient novelties" as "giants, dwarfs, fat boys, animals and other attractions." (Barnum adds that since he was catering to a Quaker clientele, he was careful to avoid anything that might seem objectionable.)[8] Looking back, again, from the perspective of Jane Jacobs, central Philadelphia presented to the walking traveler a supreme example of mixed use, a trait Jacobs has taught us to prize, as being essential to the interest and vitality of urban spaces.

Another dimension to the experience of walking in central Philadelphia that is almost never described by travelers in a deliberate and explicit way is rather figured forth with words like "promenade." To walk was not simply to get somewhere and it was not simply to see the physical sights along the way. It was to be seen and to be among others who wished to be seen. When Lieutenant Colonel Maxwell speaks of well-dressed females and compliments the street scene by comparing it to Milan, he is responding to that dimension of street life.

John F. Watson, in his *Annals of Philadelphia*, records a piece of doggerel, unattributed, seemingly from the late nineteenth century, that makes the point, with no subtlety at all.

> In vain may Bond street, or the Parks,
> Talk of their demoiselles and sparks –
> Or Boulevard's walks, or Tuileries' shades
> Boast of their own Parisian maids;
> In vain Venetia's sons may pride
> The masks that o'er Rialto glide;
> And our own Broadway, too, will sink
> Beneath the Muse's pen and ink;
> While Chestnut's fav'rite street will stand
> The pride and honour of our land![9]

The claim in the verse that Chestnut Street had come to equal the great promenades of Europe was, on the face of it, chauvinistic and hyperbolic. Certainly nothing in an American city of the nineteenth century could duplicate the subtle, complex, and serene customs of the major European centers, where conspicuous gentility had its traditional forms. The verse, moreover, does not suggest the contradictory unease Americans have generally felt in superimposing upon our indigenous egalitarian ideals the cultivation of an elite and conspicuously leisured class. Still, the existence of the verse as an exercise in popular bravado indicates how far the principal walking streets of central Philadelphia had changed. It seemed not altogether preposterous to imagine that Chestnut Street rivaled Bond Street and the Tuileries.

Richard Bushman has analyzed the stages by means of which the genteel world of the larger and more prosperous American cities came to overlay the coarse, commercial world which was already there, without replacing it. The streets that most easily changed in such a way were the ones that radiated outward from the public buildings and the seats of power. Further, there was the addition of amenities, the planting of trees, for example, that gave to those promenade streets the look of leisure and comfort.[10] The existence of women on the streets, walking apparently in a not particularly purposeful way, elegant, beautiful, happy to be admired was an often remarked feature of mid-nineteenth-century urban life. Their presence required streets that had become free of much threat of soil, without much rudeness and physical menace, with a happy tolerance of what was, sometimes, a low-grade flirtation ritual. During a mid-nineteenth-century tour, the geologist and polymath Sir Charles Lyell returned to Philadelphia after spending some months in the South. What struck him first was the quality and refinement of the street life, "the well-dressed people walking on the neat pavements, under the shade of a double row of green trees, or gazing, in a bright, clear atmosphere, at the tastefully arranged shop windows." [11] A complex and troubled city at midcentury, there was still an arena of refinement in the

Figure 4. The density of pedestrian traffic on an ordinary day on Market Street in the late 1920s. Courtesy of the Library Company of Philadelphia.

principal central streets that almost inevitably struck the imagination of travelers and invited them to join it.

Walking in Philadelphia, noticing that other people walk, responding to that custom with a certain pleasure and wonder—all of that remains quite strikingly consistent as the nineteenth century gives way to the twentieth. The city's ethnic population had grown enormously by the early years of the twentieth century, along with a huge increase in the city's industrial production, especially the vast sweatshops located largely in the near Northeast, along the Delaware River. But the pleasures of walking in the old city are not really modified by the transformations of the larger city around that core. Often tense and uneasy, the city was beginning to decay faster than it built; and it had begun to demonstrate, notoriously, that it was incapable of governing itself. But the tone with which writers from elsewhere describe walking in the city remains a happy one, without irony or indirection.

If there is a single feature that connects those walking tours, in the nineteenth and early twentieth century, it is the tendency to observe and record the small details of the physical city. The pavement, writes Lieutenant Colonel Maxwell, is mostly "laid with blocks of wood instead of stone." Tyrone Power records the greenness of the shutters. Fanny Kemble remarks on the whiteness of the marble, the redness of the brick.[12] In 1906, Charles Henry White wrote a version of a walking tour of Philadelphia.

The sidewalks are in dovetailed bricks, and the cobblestones under the pressure of many generations now rise and fall in many delightful hollows. The weather-beaten facades of the houses are rapidly shedding their coat of paint, revealing bricks in checker-board design, bleached to a delicate salmon, with here and there soft golden umbers and liquid grays—the color quality of a faded tapestry.[13]

It is a version of the city as aesthetic object; and there is no mistaking the position of the observer, walking the streets of the old city.

In 1913, Edward Hungerford published his captivating *The Personality of American Cities*. It is ingratiating in its style, eccentric in its approach. One chapter is given to Philadelphia. If what Hungerford finds to say about Philadelphia seems to avoid some hard truths about a difficult and intractable city, what he says is not, for that reason, false. His route is the road through Chestnut Hill, perhaps the city's most comfortable neighborhood, then and now. Never mind that he sees no foundries, no clothing factories, and no docks. What he sees makes him happy, alive, observant. And most of what he observes is done on foot.

The distance of his approach is remarkable. He begins his description at the William Penn Inn, which still stands and flourishes, in what is now called Gwynned, an area that seems like the exurbs, a long distance from the center of the city, some twenty miles, a distance no one would dream of walking now. If others of another age approached the city from the river, Hungerford prefers to approach it from one of the pikes that radiate outward. Someone fortunate and affluent enough to own an automobile might choose to drive into the city. Someone else, neither fortunate nor affluent, might choose to seek out the necessary trolley lines. For his part, Hungerford chooses to walk. "So from the William Penn Inn one may start after breakfast as one might have started a century ago–to walk his way into the busy town."

Everything along the way suggests the field of vision of a person on foot: Quaker gravestones, lunch at a roadside tavern, a milepost. Moving through Chestnut Hill, Mount Airy, and Germantown, he reads the historic plaques along the way, musing on the events they commemorate. Not only a walker, a dawdler, a connoisseur of the sidewalk, he is finally defeated by unvarying rows of brick houses as the congested part of the city begins to close around him, and he catches a trolley. Giving a passing acknowledgment to the sordid streets of the unfashionable parts of the city, he is, in due course, beyond them and happy to leave the trolley. "'Arch street,' calls the conductor and it is time to get out. It is time to thread your way down one of the earliest streets of the old Red City...." Back to the sidewalk, he reads epitaphs, lingers over store windows, muses on the allure of the parks.[14]

It is a mode of walking that Philadelphia seems to encourage, not very directional or purposive, alert to the emanations of the past, fond of the self-enclosed scene, especially the miniature. George Barton was a master of the mode in his *Little Journeys around Old Philadelphia* (1926): "If we stroll a block farther north to Willing's Alley we can find our way amid skyscrapers to the iron gateway that leads to old St. Joseph's, and entering therein enjoy the calm repose that is so foreign to the screeching age."[15] But the absolute master of the mode for the first third of the twentieth century was Christopher Morley, not a visitor, not quite a native, a sensibility that seemed, for a time, to be utterly adjusted

to the surviving style of the old city—elegant, a little dilettantish and
overripe, lightly erudite, witty, self-derogating yet unmistakably pleased
with himself.

Morley describes himself moving through the life of Philadelphia
streets. He walks, he passes, he finds his way, he prowls; he dodges and
darts along; he hurries, threads, navigates; he loiters; again and again
he strolls. In one of his essays, directed specifically toward the pleasures
of walking, he confesses himself a saunterer and makes his way to
Washington Square, a copy of *Walden* in hand, where he annotates the
city with all of the attention of Thoreau at Walden Pond. The essay is
filled with sky and sun and light. It is filled with other people: "The most
interesting persons are always those who have nothing special to do:
children, nurses, policemen, and actors at 11 o'clock in the morning."
And it is filled with that specialty of walks in Philadelphia, the unexpected, framed view: a doorway, a portion of a house, an urban garden.

A kindly observer in the Dreer seed warehouse, which backs upon Orange
street, noticed me prowling about and offered to take me up in his elevator. From
one of the Dreer windows I had a fascinating glimpse down upon these roofs and
gardens. One of them is the rear yard of the Italian consulate at 717 Spruce street.
Another is the broader garden of the Catholic Historical Society, in which I noticed with amusement Nicholas Biddle's big stone bathtub sunning itself. Then
there is the garden of the adorable little house at 725 Spruce street, which is
particularly interesting because, when seen from the street, it appears to have no
front door. The attic window of that house is just our idea of what an attic window ought to be.[16]

There are aspects of Morley's mode of sauntering that we will not see
again. It is related to the associative, richly responsive style of literary
walking that the English Romantics found so congenial. And it is a part
of a tradition of the man of letters, the essay constructed so as to seem
like the tip of the iceberg, light and apparently effortless, merely suggesting the cultivation and the erudition beneath the surface. Needless
to say, no North American city, perhaps no city anywhere, is ever again
likely to be represented as being so nonthreatening and nonproblematic
as Morley's Philadelphia. But the point, of course, is not to notice that
Morley is dated but to notice that the nature of Philadelphia, for a long
time, provided the density and intricacy of texture that was the subject
matter for his peripatetic essays.

For all of the erosions of urban life, Philadelphia is still a walking
city and visitors recognize the fact, even now, often with more than a

little wonder. In 1989, Bill Bryson published his account of a cross-country journey, after having lived abroad for a number of years, beginning at his home city of Des Moines and driving to both coasts and back. With a stance of something like feigned innocence and a virtuoso wise-guy tone, Bryson occasionally discovers the nobility of roadside America; mostly he notes its appalling vulgarity. At a point, he stops in Philadelphia.

Parking his car near City Hall, he muses on what he knows about the incompetence and corruption of the city. But in a page or two, he has begun to enjoy the city, to enter into its intimate life. And the place at which he has begun to do this is significant: he has parked his car and, willingly forgetting all of the stories he has ever read and heard about Philadelphia's abysmal city government, he has begun to walk. Out from behind his car windows, Philadelphia begins to seduce him. The city, he discovers, "had skyscrapers and there was steam rising through vents in the sidewalk and on every corner stood a stainless steel hot-dog stand, with a chilly-looking guy in a stocking cap bobbing around behind it." [17]

The report of his experience of Philadelphia is quick and witty, like everything else in the book more sardonic than affectionate. But the verbs give it away, the real feeling for the day in Philadelphia; they are as specific to the nature of the city as the verbs of Christopher Morley. He "wandered over." He "ambled along." He "found my way." The two places that impress him most are Fairmount Park and the urbane and comfortable neighborhood of Mount Airy; both of them delight him with the ways in which they provide a sensory ambiance for a ground-level experience of the city.

"For all its incompetence and criminality, Philadelphia is a likable place," writes Bryson. "For one thing, unlike Washington, it feels like a big city." Again, it is the verb that gives the tone away. No place "feels like a big city" when one is coming in for a landing in a plane, riding through on a train, or driving in a car. "Looks like," perhaps, but not "feels like." The impulse to walk in Philadelphia is implicit, understood, and difficult to articulate. But it is not to be taken for granted: it represents a subtle complex of characteristics by no means shared by most American cities in the distant past and shared by very few of them now.

3

Mythic Places

E very city of any size or age has, as a dimension of its identity, a body of myth. It is odd, perhaps, how narrow the possibilities are for such urban myths. Any city newspaper, virtually every day, will contain a prominent story of flamboyant crime, incredible endurance, extraordinary heroism, acts of imaginative and creative daring. Many of these might become the stuff of legend, remembered, told, embellished, attached to the very nature of the city. But few of them endure, either locally or in a wider arena. Beginnings and endings, or endings narrowly averted, often do have the power to remain in the collective mind in a formulaic, legendary way. Peter Minuit, with tall hat and blunderbuss, buys Manhattan from the local Indians for twenty-four dollars; Mrs. O'Leary's cow kicks over the lantern and Chicago nearly disappears in flames. Supremely, it is events that seem to have a bearing on the nature and destiny of American history that can come to carry a mythic charge. Gettysburg matters as a destination, a shrine, a great mythic repository; Mechanicsburg, a few miles away, does not because it is interesting only in a local way. It is clear, whether explicit or not, that travelers to Philadelphia have always looked both for those sites that seem to define the special quality of the city and those locations that mark events with a national import.

The capacity of a myth to resonate, over time and beyond its place of origin, is, to a large extent, mysterious and ineffable. Irony, dramatic flair, and a quality that might be called historical pathos have something to do with the power of those myths that endure, that and a large measure of chance. Still, there are dimensions of certain myths that are altogether obvious, features that account for the extent and the limits of their particular durability. Consider Franklin's reputed "discovery" of the electricity of lightning by flying a kite in a thunderstorm.

One aspect of the energy of the story is its emblematic nature: a quintessential early American reveals a principle of the natural world by an action that is seemingly spontaneous, amateur, whimsical, and quite reckless. There is a requisite legendary quality to the story, larger than life, told and retold, pictured but not written. Insofar as a picture does enter the mind, it is a charming one–the glasses, the powdered wig, the benign expression, the key, and the kite. Still, Franklin and the kite is quite a limited bit of national lore, partly because it feels vernacular, like those preposterous stories invented by Parson Weems about Washington, the cherry tree, the silver dollar, perpetuated through the centuries by a folk tradition. Indeed, it is true that nothing in the biographies of Franklin reinforces or authenticates the story. Even its significance was always unclear and remains so now. Who could say what it meant to have "discovered" electricity in the 1750s? But at least as important as these limits of the power of the event is the absence of a location. Few people could say whether the great key-and-kite episode is supposed to have happened in Philadelphia, near Philadelphia, or somewhere else. And although a small plaque at 19 South Tenth Street purports to commemorate the key and the kite (and a huge and rather startling sculpture by Isamu Noguchi at the approach to the Benjamin Franklin Bridge memorializes it), no place in the city is actively remembered for the event and no guidebook to the city has ever pointed a traveler to such a place.

The founding of the city is probably the most distinct of those events with a high mythic import, specific to Philadelphia but with national implications, that survives almost exclusively as a tableau. A complicated series of events, involving the granting of the royal charter, the arrival, the landing, the survey of the area, the treaty with the Indians, and a multitude of planning decisions, the process now offers itself up to the ordinary person, resident or visitor, if at all, as a picture. There is the sweetly naive painting of Edward Hicks and the splendid composition of Benjamin West, both done nearly a century after the fact. Following West there are scores of engravings and reproductions derivative of his design. Different as they are, all of those images reduce the founding of the city to a frozen moment–the Indians looking gentle and accepting, Penn looking wise and magnanimous, the figures all quite placed and arranged, the bustling river in the near background and the infant city receding into the distance.

A traveler in the nineteenth century, hoping to find the place where Penn landed and signed his treaty, would have been directed to a fairly specific place on the waterfront where a legendary elm stood until 1810,

since 1827 a stone obelisk. Almost no travelers ever recorded having
gone there. More recently a statue of Penn and several bronze tablets
mark the place. "The Great Elm of Shackamaxon is the site under which
William Penn and the Delaware Indians are said to have made the great
treaty . . . ," begins one of them. But the place and the events always have
had large elements of the fictive and the site never emerged as a destination or a sacred place. Still nominally a park, the purported location
of the landing, in an area of decaying wharves and in the shadow of an
immense vacant sugar refinery, offers little to the visitor. The founding
of Philadelphia, that is, is not inscribed in the city for the traveler to
see; its plot is not available to him. Insofar as it can be held in the mind
at all, the founding of the city is most likely to be imagined as a group
picture, the heavy Quaker dress of Penn's party contrasting with the
loincloths of the Indians, all the elements of the composition turning
toward the scroll at the center.

That static, posed way of *imagining* places and events with a considerable mythic charge from the more-or-less legendary past turns
out to be so essential a way of comprehending the great sites of Philadelphia that living travelers visiting real scenes of the city often cast
them into a tableau, as if it were only possible to conceptualize them
by freezing their elements into an imagined group painting. Caroline
Gilman, author of children's books and commentator on middle-class
domestic life, reports on her visit to Philadelphia in her still quite captivating *The Poetry of Travelling in the United States.* It is the late 1830s
and she responds first, quite lyrically, to the waterworks and the Schuylkill valley.

Moving on to Philadelphia's charitable institutions, she stops first at
the asylum for the insane at the Pennsylvania Hospital.[1] Only two para-
graphs long, the passage is charming and ingratiating, without a trace of
the problematic; and it is highly visual, particularized, posed. "As we
were going through the kitchen, the neatness of which is remarkable,
my attention was arrested by a smiling looking personage, who was
boasting that he had just crossed the Red Sea with the Israelites." She
moves on and a reader now cannot help noticing the transition, because it sounds as if it were a slide show in a darkened auditorium and
she were about to move to another Kodachrome projection. "The scene
changes now, and I am at the Deaf and Dumb Asylum. . . ." Having
drawn a moral, she makes a picture:

Five girls, and an equal number of boys, were exercised in transferring each other's thoughts, conveyed by motions of the hands, to the black board; the ease with which they communicate their ideas, the accuracy of the spelling, even the variations of expression, with which they conjugate verbs, compare adjectives, &c. &c., are singularly interesting; and the kindness with which they aid each other when they detect inaccuracies, was not lost on one, who, like me, considers an affectionate impulse of the heart worth all intellectual treasures.[2]

It is a touching visit to Philadelphia, susceptible, devoid of defenses. Without irony, without any interest in intellectualizing anything she sees, she transforms everything she visits into a picture. Somehow, it seems essential, as a condition of her sentimental temperament, that Gilman do so. No one is ever sentimental about ideas and institutions, streets and buildings; one is sentimental about people caught in the vignettes of daily life, frozen moments of pathos.

At the opposite pole from Caroline Gilman, Harriet Martineau visits the city's charitable institutions with an immensely intelligent, ironic temperament. Less willing than Gilman to draw close and "paint" the inmates in a group picture, she is no less willing to take the asylums and the hospitals as demonstrable indications of the moral health of the national culture. "The insane in Pennsylvania hospital, Philadelphia, should be removed to some more light and cheerful abode, and be much more fully supplied with employment, and with stimulus to engage in it." The Asylum for the Blind in Philadelphia, on the other hand, pleases her because of the cheerful spirits of the inmates. In general, the fault of institutions for the blind is that "mirth is not sufficiently cultivated, and religion too exclusively so."[3]

Philadelphia being Philadelphia, the range of places that beckon to the traveler are not only considerable but loaded, usually, with cultural baggage. Early in the nineteenth century, it was not only the second city but "the Athens of America." Ever since, its places have often been imagined to speak for American origins, American tastes, and American moral energy. Almost nothing in the city seems to be observed simply out of curiosity, for its own sake. Almost everything has a kind of emblematic implication. As for the range of places visited, the English traveler Emily Faithfull, touring in the eighties, can provide an example. She subtitles her chapter on Philadelphia "The Quaker city–Changes in society–School of young Lady Potters–New Century Club–The Mint, and women employed in it–Theatres and English artists–Silk culture–Mr.

George W. Childs, the *Ledger*, and his work-people—Wooton—Original manuscripts and autographs—Walt Whitman: his views on New York, Boston, Washington, and the West—Mrs. Hannah Smith and the Temperance Union—Coffee-houses."[4] Along the way, a Philadelphia bronchial infection leads her to muse on "what America furnishes in this pleasing direction." Still, for all of the range of possible places to see, there is quite a narrow list of obligatory destinations. And the most compelling, for every reason, is the State House, later Independence Hall.

From the start, the building was iconic. Ubiquitously portrayed, it was the preeminent image in the mind of the traveler to Philadelphia before the fact. Seeing it often evoked a frisson, a thrill of recognition, or if not that then a sober confirmation that the building of the prints and the magazine illustrations was really, concretely *there*. Unlike those legendary events that may or may not have happened somewhere in Philadelphia, leaving the traveler with no place to visit if he wished to, those gatherings of some of the finest minds of the Enlightenment took place at a site supremely specific, and the rhythm of a busy commercial street has always moved past it. It has always been, in other words, not a preserved historical space, maintained with effort and artifice, but an address on Chestnut Street. Inside the building, its rooms have always invited the imaginative devising of a tableau, the visitor being implicitly invited to fill those rooms with the great figures of the first days of the Republic.

Yet travelers in the nineteenth century often do not respond to Independence Hall, or, responding to it, they condescend to it. The Scottish traveler James F. W. Johnson, visiting in mid-nineteenth century, names the essential destinations of the city at that time: "the celebrated Penitentiary, and the Fairmount Water-works," Girard College, and, supremely, the State House. But, if he does actually visit the State House, he does not record his having done so.[5] The encyclopedist William Chambers, an enthusiast about many things, goes flat when describing the building: "It is a respectable, old-fashioned looking brick structure, consisting of a ground and upper story, with a spire partly of wood rising from the centre, and a wing added to each end."[6] Anthony Trollope, a novelist of considerable precision, lingers for a mere three sentences—sentences, moreover, of conspicuous gracelessness—over the State House, not at first altogether certain of what was done there and when. "It was, however, here, in this building at Philadelphia, that the independence of the Union was declared in 1776, and that the constitution of the United States was framed."[7]

Part of what is at issue in understanding how a visitor, or anyone, responds to Independence Hall is the shifting fortunes of the building itself. Early nineteenth-century views, sightings along Chestnut Street, sometimes show the building crowded by nondescript commercial establishments, detracting from its definition. For a period in the early nineteenth century, its steeple had decayed and was removed; and engravings of the building in that state reveal how diminished it was, how squat and ignorable. For two centuries, it has undergone cycles of decay and desecration, preservation and respect. And its status as a shrine could hardly be said to have existed before the visit of Lafayette in 1824, the restoration of the Assembly Room in the thirties, and a succession of visiting eminences in the years immediately following. It was not until

Figure 5. The Assembly Room at Independence Hall in 1875. The experience of the room invites reverence and respect, hence the attention to hats. The man in the center of the view holds his while the woman to the right seems to rebuke the man in her field of vision who has not removed his. Still, the room offers little more drama or focus to the traveler than chairs behind velvet ropes. Courtesy of Urban Archives, Temple University, Philadelphia.

1846 that the Assembly Room was permanently opened as a museum
for the general public.[8] Clearly, trying to discover an appropriate sense
of the significance of the building before mid-nineteenth century was
difficult for a variety of physical and circumstantial reasons that made
the building more diffuse and less focused, more ordinary and less assertive than it has come to be. One would expect that the signing of
the Declaration of Independence would have hallowed the building in
which it was done. "But the unpleasant truth seems to be," writes Basil
Hall, visiting in the 1820s, "that nothing whatsoever is venerated in
America merely on account of its age, or, indeed, on any other account."
The original interior of the room, its paneling and its ornamentation,
have been pulled down, Hall reports, and "in their places, tame plaster-
ing and raw carpentry have been stuck up, on the occasion of some recent festival."[9]

In midcentury, R. A. Smith published his guidebook *Philadelphia
as It Is in 1852*, making clear its rationale in its opening pages. Existing guidebooks, of which there were many, were, he thought, dull and
uninviting. His, on the contrary, was not only enlivened with profuse
illustrations, the descriptive writing was meant to be vivid and colorful.
Still using both names, he turns first to "the State House, or Independence Hall." He moves through the essential details of design, construction, and renovation. And then he fixes the reader's attention on the
east room.

There are places which possess, in a particular degree, the power of awaking
sensations in the mind. In their effect, we acknowledge the influence which has
been so beautifully designated, the "magic of a scene." . . . Everything in the room
leads the mind back to the memorable time–to that decisive act, which has consecrated this room to undying fame. We see those patriotic men pondering on
the magnitude of the step about to be taken. Some of them seem to waver. Silence–deep and solemn silence, reigns throughout. See "that aged man" arise.
He "casts a look of inexpressible interest and unconquerable determination" on
his fellow patriots. He addresses them. Hear him![10]

It is as if Smith recognizes that the experience of Independence Hall–the
building, the room, the furnishings, and the knowledge of the events that
happened there–will not come together in a single, dramatic impression without help. His is, after all, a commercial guidebook and his
breathlessly enthusiastic tableau is meant to mediate between an empty
room with its historical associations and a popular clientele. If his at-

tempt seems vulgar, it is worth remembering that finer minds than his found the experience fragmented and unremarkable.

One way of understanding the distance between those nineteenth-century travelers who found their way to Independence Hall and the readers of Smith's guidebook is to recover the sense of the word "tourist." Throughout the nineteenth century, published reports of travels by visitors with a practiced eye and a polished style—Mrs. Trollope, Thomas Hamilton, Caroline Gilman—are reports by travelers, not tourists. Smith's guidebook, like a hundred since, is directed to tourists, a nineteenth-century word and a nineteenth-century concept. Forty years after Smith, guidebooks attained a standard that has defined their nature ever since. In 1893, Karl Baedeker edited and published the first of his guides to the United States, namely *The United States with an Excursion into Mexico: Handbook for Travellers*. Not only are the classic destinations evoked, but the ways to get there—the walks, the trains, the streetcars—are described with a particularity no tour book had ever contained before. Still, for all of that Germanic precision, the chambers of Independence Hall are quite sensuously rendered. Clearly there are implicit needs being ministered to in Smith and, overwhelmingly, in Baedeker, needs never felt by the great improvisatory travel writers of the first half of the century.

John F. Sears sets the novelty of tourism in its historical context.

Tourism requires a population with the money and the leisure to travel, an adequate means of transportation, and conditions of reasonable safety and comfort at the places people go to visit. It also demands a body of images and descriptions of those places—a mythology of unusual things to see—to excite people's imaginations and induce them to travel. These requirements were not fully met in America until the 1820s.[11]

It has never been impossible for a visitor of imagination to respond with feeling and understanding to the State House, whatever the condition of the building. But it was not always easy to do so and it was certainly not easy for that new kind of visitor in the mid-nineteenth century, the tourist. Smith's book, and later Baedeker's, participates in the transformation of the building and its implicit mythology into that new site on the American scene, a tourist attraction.

Words like "desire" and "fulfillment" come easily to mind as one tries to focus on the tourist's mode of visiting famous places. So do such religious words as "consecration" and "shrine." Remembering Smith's tableau of the Assembly Room, one can see how heavy it is with the accents of a particular species of religiosity—the crisis experience, the climactic rhetoric, the charismatic leader. Secular or quasi-religious, the tourist's experience is sensuous, at once personal and communal.

Dean MacCannell's clever and original study *The Tourist* marks out the stages by means of which a place becomes an object of the tourist's desire. Throughout his book, MacCannell uses the words of sacrament and ritual common to a religious community, making implicitly clear what he sometimes makes quite explicit, that tourist destinations, in a largely secular culture, have the capacity to serve as sacred objects. The first stage of what MacCannell calls "sight sacralization" is a naming phase, in which the object is set off from others like it; it is authenticated and a large amount of institutional support is given to clarifying the special value that the experience of the object will bring to the observer. The second stage is the "framing and elevation phase." The object is bounded, framed, fenced, enclosed in glass, guarded. In a further stage, the sacred object is enshrined, enclosed within a larger space, with lights perhaps, pedestals, the apparatus of the holy. Finally, there are mechanical reproductions of the sacred object—prints, photographs, models—and social reproduction, the naming of groups or regions after the sacred object.[12]

Reading MacCannell, one understands why Independence Hall, whatever its condition, failed so often to engage visitors at a complex intellectual and emotional level. Whatever the state of its disrepair or restoration, it was insufficiently sacralized, set off, framed, guarded, explained, and reproduced. Magazine illustrations in the nineteenth and twentieth centuries had been useful in confirming for readers the look and existence of the building. But they did not sacralize it. Seeing the building, or its east room, on its site was insufficient to fulfill a wish for a kind of mythic, patriotic thrill. Utterly authentic, the building was, paradoxically, insufficiently authenticated in all of those visual and cultural ways that MacCannell lists. Outside and inside, the building was a picture, two dimensional, without depth. It was not a tableau. Smith labors to make it one—the hushed anticipation, the bodies bent to the task, the electrifying words, the courage and defiance of the faces. But the ordinary visitor could not have supplied the sacred scene from his own imagination.

Seventy-five years after Smith's re-creation of the drama of the Assembly Room, the popular journalist Frederick Lewis published his tour of the city. It is another of those useful reference points, laying out the lure of the city, in the twenties, for the middlebrow readers of *Women's Home Companion*. Drawn to aspects of Philadelphia, Lewis also distances himself from its density and clutter, another in that long tradition of essays about cities written by people who do not like cities very much.

At one point, he recommends several items of local cuisine, with a kind of fussy niceness appropriate to his audience and, one assumes, his own sense of the decencies. "The big hotels serve these dishes well and expensively; but the best way to get them in true Philadelphia style is in the ordinary cafes along the main streets. You can't go far wrong on these places if you stick to the clean-looking ones." In due course, he turns to the great historic buildings. Independence Hall he finds impressive, noble, with "the finest public interiors in America." The historic chambers possess "the intimate qualities of a very fine home."

Contemplating the Assembly Room, he imagines the events of 1776.

Here is the dandified Hancock signing his life away in bold defiance of the English king. Here is Jefferson, that gentle man, entering the chamber from his corner house not many blocks away, bearing the manuscript which makes us free. Here is Charles Carroll of Carrollton signing his name at full length lest among so many Charles Carrolls he might be saved from the danger which his fellow signers had bravely incurred.[15]

The rhetoric of immediacy, the tone of willed wonder, it all seems scarcely different from R. A. Smith writing in 1852. Lewis probably did not know that bringing the Assembly Room to life has been an exercise with a century of familiarity behind it. What he did know was that something more dramatic than the room itself is necessary to energize the mythic power of Independence Hall and that the best means to this end was the creation of another tableau.

Not very many responses to the historical buildings of Philadelphia in the twentieth century, by traveling foreigners or by Americans from elsewhere, avoid the formulaic. Again Henry James does. For all of the eccentricity of the occasion of *The American Scene* and its mandarin style, it provides perhaps the single response to Independence Hall in the twentieth century that is serious, reflective, and complex.

James records the "news" about Independence Hall, noting ironically that it is news only for him—that he should have lived so long and known so much and still not know this!—that Independence Hall is a building of immense and utterly captivating charm. As if he were a phenomenologist of the Geneva school of fifty years later, he tries to discover and compose into words the consciousness of being within that space, musing over the interplay between his moving through those great chambers, a pilgrim in 1906, and the intensity of the pastness of the building. And he reflects on the intimacy and the human scale of the building, set within a culture increasingly given to valuing bigness. He even does his version of a tableau, although like no one else's.

The old ghosts, to our inward sensibility, still make the benches creak as they free their full coat-skirts for sitting down; still make the temperature rise, the pens scratch, the papers flutter, the dust float in the large sun-shafts; we place them as they sit, watch them as they move, hear them as they speak, pity them as they ponder, know them, in fine, from the arch of their eyebrows to the shuffle of their shoes.[14]

James ends the passage with a wonderfully evocative description of the light and shade, the mellow Philadelphia morning, as it filters through the great building. Reading James, one realizes that almost no one else writes about visiting Independence Hall as if trying to capture the inner experience of actually being there.

Thinking about the difficulty of focusing on a building, a room, and the political abstractions that were conceived there, one understands, after the fact, what was needed: an object with a smaller visual field than the building and its rooms, crisp, clear, and uncomplicated, yet fluid and ambivalent, free-floating in its signification. No one could ever have guessed that a broken bell would have filled that need. But of course it did.

The history of the Liberty Bell is strange and extraordinary in the stages by which it took on the status of an icon. In some respects its appeal is quite obvious. Unlike the State House itself, the bell could be set off and framed, placed on a pedestal, lit. Unlike the State House, it could travel the country by rail, to be seen and touched by thousands along the way. And as for setting it off in its own consecrated space, the bell is indeed now housed in its own building, with its own guide staff. Unlike the State House, or Independence Hall, built for one purpose, used for several more, the naming of the bell is perfectly clear. It is called the Liberty Bell because it proclaimed liberty: the words on the bell even say so. Unlike the State House, which could only be pictured, the bell could be reproduced in a dizzying multitude of forms. It has appeared as a logo for innumerable commercial products, organizations, and causes;

VESTIBULE, INDEPENDENCE HALL.

Figure 6. Despite its stark setting in 1875, the Liberty Bell was center of attention in the entry to Independence Hall. Courtesy of Urban Archives, Temple University, Philadelphia.

pictures of it have appeared on stamps, coins, matchbooks, political buttons, and savings bond posters; miniature scale models of it in metal and plastic have ornamented mantels, windowsills, and curio shelves for a century and a half; a current telephone directory reveals Liberty Bell Cleaners, Liberty Bell Cycle, Liberty Bell Fuel Oil, Liberty Bell Restaurant, Liberty Bell Steak Co., and Liberty Bell Towing.

The history of the bell is, by now, well known, both its history as a made object, cast in a particular place, mounted, rung, cracked—and its vernacular history, the sum of the things generally believed to be true about it. Guides and guidebooks make no attempt to conceal those elements of its popular history that would seem to diminish its totemic status. Yet its power to attract and move remains intact. No one knows what liberties were the intended reference in the quotation from Leviticus: "Proclaim liberty throughout all the land unto all the inhabitants thereof." Presumably it was religious, not political liberty that was meant in 1752. One thing certain is that no reference could have been intended to the specific events of the American Revolution and the Declaration of Independence, that document being twenty-four years in the future at the time of the casting of the bell. The ringing of the bell was not reserved for dramatic occasions of patriotic import; it seems to have rung frequently, to the point of annoyance. It did not ring to announce the signing of the Declaration of Independence. And it did not crack as a result of too much enthusiasm by the bell ringer for the cause of liberty.

In 1824, a Philadelphia newspaper story claimed that the bell had been the first to announce the signing of the Declaration of Independence, seemingly the first such claim. But the decisive support for the sacralizing of the bell came from a story by George Lippard, the same George Lippard of the muckraking *Quaker City*. Appearing in the *Saturday Courier* for January 2, 1847, and frequently reprinted, the story tells of a white-haired man and, by his side, a "flaxen-haired boy, with laughing eyes of Summer blue," who wait in the steeple of the State House while the Continental Congress debates the Declaration. The old man sends the boy to listen outside the chamber and to bring word of the Congress's decision. After much impatient waiting, the old man hears a merry laugh outside.

There, among the crowds on the pavement, stood the blue-eyed boy, clapping his tiny hands, while the breeze blowed his flaxen hair all about his face.

And then, swelling his little chest, he raised himself on tiptoe, and shouted the single word–

"RING!"

Lippard's fiction, widely popular in its own right, was certified by two quasi-official works of the time, Benson J. Lossing's *Field Book of the Revolution* (1848) and Joel Tyler Headley's *Life of George Washington* (1854), both of which repeated the story without reservation. The legend was even transformed into verse, included in a school primer, and widely memorized as a piece of parlor recitation.

Hushed the people's swelling murmur,
    Whilst the boy cries joyously;
"Ring!" he's shouting, "ring, grandfather,
    Ring! Oh, ring for Liberty!"[15]

In the time since that overheated melodrama, we have come to understand better than we used to what happens when we think about, or visit, or sensually encounter a mythically loaded artifact. Dean Mac-Cannell writes of the moment in which a tourist comes face to face with an attraction, recognizes it, and participates in the ritual of being there. It is not unusual that such a moment be accompanied by what Mac-Cannell calls "'truth' markers." One learns, perhaps, that certain features of the famous place are folklore, pure invention, bogus. But such knowledge does not undermine the veneration for the place; it simply adds a level of privileged knowledge to the pleasures of being there.[16] For the tourist who approaches the Liberty Bell naively, it turns out to look just like its pictures and it speaks, in a powerfully physical way, to the precise moment of American independence. To a tourist who does know the history of the bell, not a difficult knowledge to come by since a small, quite candid history of the bell is sold at the Independence Hall bookshop, the power of the bell may very well not really be diminished, debunked, or undermined. It is, if MacCannell is right, actually enhanced by giving the tourist, in addition to the sensuous pleasure of being there, a privileged piece of the "truth."

Still, if the bell as icon provides a framed configuration–immensely familiar before the fact, that can be walked around and touched, photographed, talked about with others, brought home in miniature replicas, all of which Independence Hall cannot as easily do–the bell is still not a universal experience for the visitors to the city, even after the point, in the mid-nineteenth century, at which it became quite clearly a sacred relic. Visitors who travel to the city and write about it, publishing their accounts–Dickens, Chambers, Beatrice Webb–do not write about the bell. It is, from the start of its fame, too much the tourist attraction: tourists, and what they do, are always condescended to by other people, including other tourists. And the bell, whether one knows its history or not, seems an easy thing to see, a hard thing to write about, in the same sinuous prose that one would give to the Schuylkill valley and the marble steps of the fashionable city.

Those great, resonant, mythic buildings, especially Independence

Hall itself, should, perhaps, always have provided the focus for anybody's tour of Philadelphia. But they have always been in competition.
In the early years of the Republic, their claim to symbolize and represent
the memory of the dramatic acts of national origin was undermined by
a lack of interest in their preservation in a faithful continuity with their
eighteenth-century character and detail. Michael Kammen remarks on
a vulgar present-mindedness in the nineteenth century, in which an aggressive disregard of the past resulted in an indifference to historical
preservation.[17] With great sweep and incisiveness Kammen describes
the multitude of places and objects and practices that came to be reposi-
tories of cultural memory—Mount Rushmore, the vogue of collecting
Americana, scores of restored historical villages. Philadelphia's great
historical buildings stood a losing chance in the competition for attention. Still, in some quite moving way, one understands, watching the tour
buses pull up to the entrance to Independence Hall, that visitors to Philadelphia really know that they are about to see a room inhabited by
the ghosts, as James put it, of that extraordinary moment in which the
United States was invented.

4

The Great Granite Experiment

It was not that Eastern State Penitentiary began to be visited upon its completion and after its first prisoners had been admitted. It began to be visited *before* it was completed. The bold originality of John Haviland, the architect, and the "Pennsylvania system" of solitary punishment, a set of reformist ideas that lay behind both the emerging penal system and the structure of the penitentiary itself, were subjects of wonder and fascination on an international scale. The English traveler Captain Basil Hall visited Philadelphia in 1827. As was the custom at the time, he toured a number of institutions: the Asylum for the Deaf and Dumb, several schools. And he visited "the new Penitentiary." Its cornerstone had been laid four and a half years earlier but it would not admit its first prisoner for some two years after Hall's visit and it would be another six years before it was finished. Still, Hall took the measure of the building in progress, thought it "not without architectural beauty," found the cost astoundingly extravagant, and mused for a substantial space on the philosophy of incarceration that lay behind it, both from having thought long and hard about the idea of the penitentiary and from a tour of Philadelphia's Walnut Street Prison.[1] There, despite appalling overcrowding, a separate wing was maintained for certain youthful offenders where they were kept in solitary confinement, and Hall was able to draw his own conclusions about the efficacy of a system that would, in due course, govern the prisoners at Eastern State, or Cherry Hill.

That the reputation of the penitentiary should have preceeded its very completion is a result of three forces. One is the historical moment in which the wedding of form to function was possible in a way rare in any building at any time. There was the *idea* of the penitentiary, a new one, decidedly American. And there was the building that gave, in every line of its drawing and every stone of its execution, a powerful and palpable concreteness to that idea. *Of course* the building was famous before it had fully come to be.[2]

Second was a complex and robust debate, which framed the fact of the penitentiary and the wish to see it. In its narrowest form, the debate was between advocates of the Auburn system of New York State and the Pennsylvania system. Reacting, quite defensibly, against the congregate system in such prisons as the Walnut Street, where prisoners of all ages, those convicted and those awaiting trial, habitual criminals and petty offenders were crowded and intermixed, both the Auburn and the Pennsylvania systems placed the avoidance of the contamination of prisoners by each other at the center of the concept. In the Auburn system, prisoners would congregate, at mealtime for example, but any kind of communication was forbidden. In the Pennsylvania system, prisoners were kept in solitary confinement from their admission to their discharge. The Auburn system permitted, in fact conceptualized, the usefulness of corporal punishment as a means to the reformation of the prisoner. In the Pennsylvania system, although physical cruelty did occur, the emphasis was rather on the introspective self-examination of the prisoner, surrounded by a Quaker regard for his individual dignity. The substitution of solitary imprisonment for corporal punishment was the conceptual center of the Pennsylvania system and it was seen at the time, as indeed it should have been, as an advance over the indisputable inhumanity of the system that had come before. That two competing systems such as these should have captured the whole debate seems curious now; that they did owes something to the channels of publicity at the time and it owes quite a bit to the infancy of the penitentiary. Adam J. Hirsch's *Rise of the Penitentiary* finds prefigurations in antiquity, but not many; the idea of imprisonment with a view to reformation is, by and large, specific to the 1820s.[3]

The standard history of Eastern State Penitentiary lists some of the visitors, not simply visitors to the penitentiary, there were thousands, but visitors who came to adjudicate between the Auburn system and the Pennsylvania system, write of their observations, and report back to their home governments.[4] There were, for example, Beaumont and Tocqueville from France, William Crawford from the London Society for the Improvement of Prison Discipline, and Dr. Nicolaus Heinrich Julius of Prussia.

What obviously gave the debate such resonance was that it implied, without articulating them, a nest of questions. At the center lies the question of whether it is possible to alter human nature in certain radical and ameliorative ways, if so how, and whether such means as could be found should be adopted as state policy. Whether or not it is possible to make people better by locking them up was, by the 1830s, both an abstract question and an experimental hypothesis. Nobody called the prisoners human subjects in a large experimental project, but that is what they were. And observers watched them with something of the fascination of a behaviorist watching mice in a maze.

Third, visiting the penitentiary became as voguish as it did for a cluster of reasons having to do with the sacralization of certain destinations in American cultural life.[5] Niagara Falls and the Hudson Valley, Mammoth Cave, and Yosemite were sublime and picturesque in all of the classic ways of the great European scenic views, and besides, they were uniquely American. In a large, diverse, and officially secular culture, they had become, in John F. Sears's phrase, "sacred places." Some of the more dramatic institutions participated in the same spirit: Sing Sing Penitentiary, the Hartford Asylum, and the Pennsylvania Hospital were seen as intense visual experiences, evocative of awe and reverence, seemingly expressive of qualities uniquely American. As Sears points out, the claims of such institutions to have contributed in some powerful and innovative way to the moral betterment of mankind was reinforced by the experience of visiting them. They were microcosms, little worlds, suggestive of the imagery of the pastoral, on the one hand, the utopian on the other. They even embodied the possibility of a ritual transformation, from a flawed existence to a reconstituted wholeness, or to read it another way, from burial to rebirth, all of it made possible through order and reason and Christian care.[6]

Reading the travelers' accounts, one is struck by the ease and naturalness of the inclusion of the penitentiary on an itinerary. Visiting the prison was not special or compartmentalized or problematic in any way. Any traveler would wish to describe what he saw there; but no traveler ever explains why he would wish to go there. It is as comfortable an excursion as a trip to the mint and far more dramatic.

Reading the accounts, one is struck, moreover, by an elaborate perspective and distancing. The penitentiary lay two miles from the center of the city and the traveler really did journey to it, with some deliberateness, approaching it at a slight elevation, surrounded by what remained, through the nineteenth century, a substantial margin of farmland. Its front wall was overwhelming and meant to be. Perhaps no other building in North America so impressed travelers with the contrast between its inside and its outside. Travelers sometimes note the approach with a dry solemnity. "It is a square granite building of great extent, with a tower at each angle, and the walls enclose a space of ten acres."[7] But often travelers "read" the front wall, trying to catch its grand intention or its presumed effect on those inside and those outside. Tocqueville and Beaumont reported to the French government: "Gigantic walls, crenellated towers, a vast gate of iron give to this prison the aspect of a vast *chateaufort* of medieval times."[8] One of the most impressive of these evocations of the view of the front of the penitentiary is that of Lieutenant Colonel Pisani, aide-de-camp to Prince Napoleon, touring America in 1861.

Cherry Hill Penitentiary is located at the entrance to the city on a bare plateau, sad and cold. The outside wall outlines a square nearly 200 meters long. The walls, with towers, are ten meters high. It is impossible to imagine a building whose outside architectural design gives a more exact idea of its purpose, and prepares the mind for what must impress him inside. When our carriages arrived in front of the low heavy door (a real prison door), the weather was cloudy and gray; gusts of a harsh and cold wind whipped the dust into swirls as high as the bare walls. One's heart quickens as he enters this terrible place of punishment.[9]

Everything about Pisani's description seems immediate, firsthand, and convincingly felt. But his rendering of the prison gates is also derivative of certain literary ways of ranking and conceptualizing experience. What the Western imagination in the late seventeenth and early eighteenth centuries called "the sublime" gives a priority to the expression of extreme height and depth, extreme light and darkness, extreme risk, extreme fear. Nature collaborates in the arena of moral threat: it is always dark when the sublime is being evoked, the door is always heavy, and the wind always swirls. Such impulses find their most potent expression in the Gothic romance, a strain of fiction undiminished from late eighteenth century to the present time. It is a complicated subgenre, largely because it embraces works of enduring quality along with the formulaic and the meretricious. But somewhere near the center of any passage of "the sublime" or any characteristic passage of Gothic romance is an affective aesthetic: the writer hopes to evoke a powerful moment of revulsion, surprise, and pleasure, the frisson. It is what Pisani works for, perhaps without knowing he is doing so, as he invites the reader to follow him through those gray, terrible walls. And thus a fragment of travel reporting reads like a page from a Gothic romance. Pisani's tone, and traces of its origin, is often found in the accounts of

Figure 7. An early lithograph of Eastern State Penitentiary, published by Childs and Inman in 1833. The setting of the prison was still rural and pastoral, the light, the sky, and the castellated towers, however, were suggestive of the Gothic and the portentous. Courtesy of the Library Company of Philadelphia.

other travelers. Caroline Gilman, for example, writes that as one approaches the massive walls and towers of the penitentiary, "a European association occurs to the mind, (such as reading furnishes,) which is rarely furnished in this country."[10]

What most defines the accounts of visits to Eastern State Penitentiary in the mid-nineteenth century, however, is the collapse of distance. Once past all of those views of the approach, the walls, the towers, once past those evocations of the mood of the place, a remarkable number of the visitors fix upon individual prisoners, develop a kind of empathy for their situation, and report the encounter with blocks of dialogue. It is a mode of travel writing familiar to us now; the writer develops the special voice of a resident of the place visited, in an anecdotal way, with an attention both to local traits and to individual oddities. Small dramatic encounters carry the burden of the reportage. However commonplace now, it is a way of writing about being somewhere that was rare in earlier periods. The norm, for the traveler to Philadelphia in the nineteenth century, is to record the *look* of a range of places in the city in a fairly painterly, static, depersonalized way.

On the contrary, although Harriet Martineau begins her chapter on the Philadelphia penitentiary by contrasting it with Auburn prison, framing the debate once again on fairly abstract grounds, she turns almost immediately to individual prisoners, grounding her consideration of the sanative power of work in what she calls "small incidents," recording a moment of interview and the rhythms of the prisoner's speech. How, she asks of a prisoner shoemaker, can he begin work so early as he claims to, on a winter morning when it is surely almost dark. "'I hammer my leather,'" he replies. "'That requires very little light. I get up and hammer my leather.'"[11] The repetition in that brief bit of dialogue is precisely pertinent. It suggests of the prisoner a tone of earnest sincerity and it suggests of Martineau a careful, even dogged fidelity to what the man actually said.

Touring the prison in the 1830s was commonplace and encouraged. But visiting cells, unescorted by a keeper, was unusual. Martineau persuaded the warden to permit her access to individual cells and she reports on a number of such encounters, casting herself as a kind of secular pastor, counseling patience, resignation, and courage. If the view of the prison walls in half-light borrows from the Gothic romance, Martineau's scenes draw upon the tradition of the sentimental novel of late eighteenth and early nineteenth century, in which the central figure moves through a succession of interactions with badly damaged people, all the while responding to them with sympathy and pathos.

"May I ask," said I to one for whom I had much regard, "may I ask what all these black marks on your wall are for?" I was not without a conjecture, remembering that he was to go out on the 17th of the next August, this being the 1st of December.

He looked down, and said he had no secret in the matter, only that I should think him very silly. I told him that I did not think any amusement silly to one who had so few.

"Well, madam, I have been trying to find out what day of the week the 17th of next August will be; but I can't quite make out, because I don't know whether the next is leap year." [12]

William Chambers surveys the domestic architecture of the city, the plan of its streets, but everything is in the middle distance and no inhabitant speaks. In due course, he visits schools, factories, the mint, a publisher, and scarcely a person emerges. But on a visit to the penitentiary, he enters the cell of a man who was perhaps thirty years old, "with a good-humoured expression of countenance, and was dressed in a linen blouse, confined around the waist." The man was imprisoned for killing his wife, in self-defense, he protests, fending off an attack by her with an ax. Chambers is struck by the injustice and the pathos of his situation and hopes that "by good conduct he might by and by obtain a remission of his sentence." [13] No one else, in a very busy chapter on Philadelphia, has captured the interest of Chambers nor engaged his sympathy.

The reasons for this collapse of distance are two. In visiting every other site of interest to the tourist, what is presented is an ensemble experience. On the street, at the mint, visiting an asylum, the traveler is among others: officials, the people within the place being visited who are going about their business while being observed, other visitors. At the penitentiary, on the other hand, visitors, at least the more eminent and insistent visitors, are locked into a cell with an otherwise solitary prisoner. The effect is immensely compelling; it seems generally to create an instant bond and an extraordinary sense of trust. Second, as I have suggested above and must repeat now, the prisoners were experimental subjects in a project of social engineering of enormous import, potential exhibits in a vast scheme of behavior modification well over a hundred years before anyone had thought to use such a phrase. Most of those

Figure 8. An etching of a cell block at Eastern State Penitentiary from
a French description of the prison in 1837. Courtesy of the Library
Company of Philadelphia.

conversational vignettes between compassionate visitor and suffering
prisoner have at their center the question of change, reform, remorse,
guilt, and transcendence, life after release. And in every encounter,
the whole grand scheme of the Pennsylvania system is confirmed or
undermined.

In the 1840s Dickens visited the penitentiary and wrote the most famous, most enduring, most powerful of all of the accounts of such a visit. His first impressions of the city are sepulchral, the tomb-like United States Bank; and his judgments are reserved, as if he were more than a little bored with a need to say something about the institutions of the city before moving on to the penitentiary, obviously his principal destination. (A member of the prison board, Richard Vaux, records Dickens as having said that there were two places in America he most wished to see, Niagara Falls and the penitentiary at Philadelphia.) [14] He has concluded before arriving at the prison, on the basis of the well-known rationale of the system itself, that the policy of solitary confinement, though well intentioned, was cruel and wrong. Seeing the penitentiary and the effects of the forced solitude on the faces of the prisoners, he is all the more convinced that "there is a depth of terrible endurance in it which none but the sufferers themselves can fathom, and which no man has a right to inflict upon his fellow-creature. I hold this slow and daily tampering with the mysteries of the brain to be immeasurably worse than any torture of the body." [15]

No one else is so attentive to the details of the prison as Dickens, the play of light and shade, the materials of construction, the oak, the stone, the iron, the effect of time written in the physical aspects of the life there, the sounds, the desperate attempts of the prisoners to fill the vacuum with some small act of the imagination. The centerpiece of Dickens's essay is a sustained series of portraits, varying in their details and the emotional charge they seek to convey and evoke but all of them searching for some kind of interiority, some empathy, some entry into the inner life of the prisoners.

Each of the profiles is remarkable, oddly observant, interactive, at once slightly comic, as if held at a distance, and immensely compassionate, as if embraced. If it were not tautological to do so, one would call the portraits Dickensian. The first of the prisoners stops his work, at the loom, when they enter, takes off his spectacles, and answers the questions of his visitors, hesitating a moment each time he speaks.

He wore a paper hat of his own making, and was pleased to have it noticed and commended. He had very ingeniously manufactured a sort of Dutch clock from some disregarded odds and ends; and his vinegar-bottle served for the pendulum. Seeing me interested in this contrivance, he looked up at it with a great deal of pride, and said that he had been thinking of improving it, and that he hoped the hammer and a little piece of glass beside it "would play music before long." He had extracted some colours from the yarn with which he worked, and

painted a few poor figures on the wall. One, of a female, over the door, he called
"The Lady of the Lake." [16]

Someone, Dickens or one of his official companions, alludes to the prisoner's wife; the prisoner shakes his head, turns aside, and covers his
face with his hands. Someone else asks whether time passes quickly.
Time, the prisoner replies, is very long. He gazes about as if he has
forgotten something, sighs heavily, puts on his spectacles, and returns
to work.

The portrait is a miniature masterpiece of the literature of sensibility, the first of several, each of them as affecting as it is because, reading them even now, one is convinced that they are, at once, a gallery of
rhetorical appeals and, at the same, a totally plausible rendering of a life
situation immeasurably miserable.

Surely there are innumerable situations in our own ugly century in
which seeing the sights and taking an ideological position are indistinguishable. But it was a rarity in the nineteenth century to find the two
purposes crowding each other, overlapping in some unavoidable way. It
was partly the novelty of Dickens's mode, partly the shock of what he
said that aroused the opposition. He was, after all, discovering an appalling cruelty in the province of the Quakers. One reaction was to ig-
nore the legitimacy of his response. Actually, ignoring the problems of
the Pennsylvania system had been the policy before Dickens arrived. In
its report to the Pennsylvania legislature in 1840, the inspectors, specifically the warden, reported that bodily health among prisoners was in no
way diminished after their admittance. And as for mental health, "We
have a number of men who have been in close confinement from four to
nine years, and three nearly ten years, whose minds have not suffered,
but have become decidedly brighter and stronger than they were on the
day of their admission." [17] In the reports through the rest of the century,
one catches a defensive note from time to time but never the slightest
admission that what Dickens said was true: for any but the most amazingly resilient prisoners, solitary imprisonment was devastating. So
compelling was the ideology of the Pennsylvania system that a century
later, long after it had been abandoned as an instrument of penology, a
historian of the penitentiary set about to defend it against Dickens's portraits of the prisoners by identifying the real prisoners whom Dickens
saw and constructing a rejoinder out of the words of the warden and the
prison's moral instructor. [18]

It is not only Dickens who is moved by the penitentiary in an uncommon and extraordinary way. Caroline Gilman is shown a specimen prisoner and his cell. She notes the light, the space, the heating, the bed-stead—and a mirror. Suddenly drawn into a sense of the ego of the prisoner, his sense of self, she contrives to see *his* world through *his* eyes.

To think of a man's watching his daily decline for twelve or twenty years in that little glass, and see the eye grow dim and the hair turn gray, and compare the laughing glance of boyhood, or the self-satisfied smile of manhood, with the withering touch of age, alone—alone! [19]

Leaving the prison, she reflects on the possibility that her compassion might be misplaced. The prisoners are prisoners, after all, because they have been duly convicted of having acted out a vice. Still, she cannot shake the image of a tiny plot of soil in the yard of a cell, which a prisoner has tended, nurturing a few flowers. And she writes a poem, narrated by the prisoner as "I," in which the flowers speak to him of regeneration, and God's grace, and the possibilities of redemption.

At least as interesting as the feelings of visitors to the penitentiary is the judgment that they came away with. Recalling the debate between the Auburn and the Pennsylvania systems, a visit to Cherry Hill invited a response that was at once emotional and intellectual. Nobody traveling to Niagara Falls or Yosemite had to decide anything. Travelers to Cherry Hill did feel obliged to adjudicate the issue, often on the basis of a very brief tour. There were few who came away without a firm opinion; and those opinions diverge in ways that are unpredictable and quite strange. A trip to Philadelphia's penitentiary was the great mirror of subjectivity for nineteenth-century American travel. Everyone obviously sees something very different from everyone else.

Thomas Brothers, for example, writes out of a political persuasion that is unregenerate Tory and a temperament that is joyless and petulant. Appalled at the public disorder and the mobocracy of the United States, he writes of his travels by way of warning Britain of the perils of reckless radicalism. He visits the penitentiary early in his travels, at a point—his travels were published in 1840—when it was at its height as an attraction and an institutional model. With his social and personal predisposition, it ought to be possible to tell, before the fact, what he would make of the prison. In fact he is outraged by it, appalled by the darkness, the isolation, the deprivation of food, the various restraining devices: the "Tranquillising Chair," the "Iron Gag." He quotes copiously both from prisoners and from official reports, leaving the experience of the peni-

tentiary with a revulsion that is at once moral and physical.[20] After the
fact, a reader can, perhaps, with some ingenuity, connect his response
to the prison with the ideology that he makes explicit at the beginning of
his book. But it is only a facile exercise in hindsight. Another Tory might
have come to opposite conclusions.

Four years later, John Robert Godley published his tours and they
are as good-natured as Brothers is dour; he makes clear at the outset
that he wishes to avoid the mean-spirited, superior, satiric tone of so
many British travelers to America. Amused by pretense and charmed by
authenticity, he moves through the landscape without tendentiousness
and with not much more by way of a framework than a happy willingness to accept a considerable range of human variety on its own terms.
Again, knowing that much of Godley's starting point, it would be impossible to guess what he would make of the penitentiary. He is, in fact,
altogether impressed by it: he describes the prisoners contentedly weav-
ing and reading, eating well, seeming to be healthy and well balanced.
And he decides that the Pennsylvania system is much preferable to the
Auburn system.[21]

The reason that reactions to the penitentiary differed in so odd and
unpredictable a way is that the penitentiary itself was contradictory
and odd; it seems less peculiar now, in retrospect, that travelers would
have differed about it than that they ever would have agreed. One looks
in vain in the words of the early theorists, the administrative figures, the
legislature, the early wardens for some trace of self-serving hypocrisy,
some blithe superiority, some kind of monstrous guile papered over
with platitudes. Nothing like that appears; they seem all to have been
well-meaning, thoughtful people, compassionate, generous of spirit. Yet
adjusting one's framework only slightly, they all begin to take on an obsessive narrowness, like terrible pilgrims in a tale by Hawthorne perhaps, undeterred by variety and complexity, driven by a cause. From our
perspective, the penitentiary can only seem to have been an extraordinarily enlightened advance over such perversions as the Walnut Street
Prison. Yet as humane space, it looks, to our eyes, like a movie set from
Fritz Lang. Only Beaumont and Tocqueville, among contemporary travelers, are caught up in the ambivalence of the penitentiary.

We have the materials to prove that the penitentiary system reforms and that it
does not reform; that it is costly and cheap; easy to administer and impracticable:
in a word, that it suits or does not suit France, according to the taste of the inter-

viewer; and we guarantee to support each of these assertions with very pertinent examples.[22]

The words are Tocqueville's and in the next paragraph he confesses that he has posed the contrarieties as he has largely in a spirit of fun. He is by no means paralyzed by the ambivalence built into the penitentiary system. And in the long run, he and Beaumont are able to make their recommendations to the French government, but always without losing sight of the terrible polarities built into the question.

They were both struck with the absence of flogging, of corporal punishment in general, as an instrument of policy at Eastern State. They were impressed with the ingenuity with which dignified forms of work were devised despite the isolation of each prisoner. They were persuaded that the separation of the prisoners from each other was beneficial to reform. To a substantial degree, however, their opinion of the system was based not simply by weighing matters of policy but by interviews with prisoners, which Tocqueville conducted, reconstructing the conversations afterward. Sensitive to their well-being, their sense of self, their mental poise, he draws them out: some are resigned, placid, self-composed, a few are in despair, at the edge of madness.

At a point, it becomes obvious that Tocqueville and Beaumont have escaped the subject matter of this book. Although there is always something of the classic traveler about them, they come to appear as they intended to be from the start, visiting scholars of an innovative penal system, intent on forming practical recommendations for the possible adaptation of that system to a very different culture. It becomes clear, reading them, if it were not clear all along, that they do not act like travelers because they are not travelers. Travelers tend to deliver a quick impression, with one eye on the sight, another eye on the itinerary, the schedule, the next sight down the road. And travelers tend to carry a mystique along with them as a mechanism for understanding the destination, a myth being, after all, the reason they wished to go there in the first place.

Both students of the penal system and travelers visited Eastern State Penitentiary into the 1850s. In his guidebook *Philadelphia as It Is in 1852*, R. A. Smith advises that tickets of admission can be obtained at the offices of any of the inspectors, adding that Mr. Vaux, president of the board, "takes pleasure in giving any information in his power respecting this truly noble Institution, which, we assure the reader, is well worthy of a visit." [23] But one feels, reading Smith's description, that his praise is slightly formulaic, his defense against attacks slightly weary, that, while the institution remained immensely impressive, the *idea* of the penitentiary had become routinized. Certainly at a local level the idea of the solitary system as an instrument of reform had been badly eroded.[24] And a national temper more wary and skeptical, more respectful of the intractable elements of human nature, had replaced the optimism and the faith in perfectability of the twenties, thirties, and forties.[25] Meanwhile, the prison remained, of course, its ideology gradually altered but its form intact. No visitor, encountering the building, would fail to be utterly startled by it. But no standard guidebook for over a century has recommended a visit to it.

Still, it was within the twentieth century that the last great rendering of the experience of the penitentiary was written and published. From midsummer 1902 to January 1903 Theodore Dreiser had lived in Philadelphia, a brief period dominated by a severe depression following the commercial failure of *Sister Carrie* and by his inability to find steady work. Still, his diaries note place names, long walks, the rudiments of the journalistic, encyclopedic experiences of new places that was so much a part of his character and his genius. In 1910, as he was beginning to plan the novel that was to become *The Financier*, he returned to the city to research in the files of the Philadelphia *Public Ledger* the career of the brokerage tycoon Charles T. Yerkes and in general the details of financial manipulation at the turn of the century. What his papers do not reveal and what his biographers do not say is that he most certainly took the occasion to refresh himself on the precise features of the city, its uncommon places, its nuances of manner and style. And when *The Financier* appeared in 1912, the local geography within the novel was faithful to the facts of the city, the domestic architecture and the small details of street life were plausible, and, although much of the temper of Dreiser's fictive city might have been appropriate to any American city of the time, it was certainly never false to Philadelphia.

After some dubious financial manipulations, Frank Cowperwood, the financier of the title, is indicted, tried, convicted, and sentenced to four and a half years imprisonment at Eastern State Penitentiary. And with the introduction of the penitentiary, the rhythm of the naturalistic detail changes. Up to that point, the details are used sparingly–a street name here, the completion of a new trolley line there–largely as "markers," reminders to the reader, tacking down the fictive world, at strategic points, to the empirical world of daily life in Philadelphia. The particular city of Philadelphia, as a complex social organism, does not really interest Dreiser very much, in the way, for example, that Paris interests Balzac, as an infinitely layered arena of difference and distinction, desire and enactment, implication and concealment. What does interest Dreiser is power and the human relationships that bear upon having it or not having it. And so there is enough of Philadelphia to remind us that the drama of the novel unfolds somewhere, not nowhere.

The density of detail concerning the penitentiary, on the contrary, is amazing. Within the first paragraph of Cowperwood's imprisonment there, we learn its street address, its architectural style, the acreage of its area, the height of its walls, their thickness at the base, the dimensions of the corridors—"forty-two feet wide from outer wall to outer wall . . . one hundred and eighty feet in length, and in four instances two stories high"—the light sources, the dimensions of the yards adjoining each cell, the dimensions of the cells, the composition of the doors, the rudiments of the social life of the prisoners, the work sites—"a bakery, a machine-shop, a carpenter-shop, a store-room, a flour-mill, and a series of gardens, or truck patches." All of this is in the first page, more or less, of the chapter.[26]

The details become less dense as the chapter proceeds, indeed they would have to be or the story could not get told. But there continues to be an obsessive particularity about the passage that suggests a consuming interest by Dreiser in the sheer differentness of being there. The image of a person of consequence adjusting to the look and feel of a striped, ill-fitting uniform is as poignant as anything in the novel.

What the biographies do not have to say is that Dreiser obviously toured the penitentiary, perhaps more than once, and that he took copious notes on the nature of the building, its institutional features, and the experience of being imprisoned there. At the appropriate time, he called them forth because Eastern State Penitentiary engaged, on a heroic, operatic scale, every thematic interest of *The Financier* in particular, Dreiser's fiction in general. In the great defining image at the beginning of *The Financier*, young Frank Cowperwood watches an aquarium tank, inhabited by a lobster and a squid, fascinated as the lobster, in due course, devours the squid. Taking the scene as a metaphor for life, Cowperwood assumes that everyone is either the eater or the eaten and resolves to be the former. Having lived out the metaphor without guilt or remorse, he is, precisely, the lobster without the squid, alone in his

aquarium, although, with several twists of irony, a power figure with no
scenario in which to enact his energies. In a Dreiserian world heavy
with sexual desire and sexual guilt, the penitentiary represents a terrible laboratory in which the desire remains but the fulfillment is impossible. In a fictive world in which self-dramatization counts for very
much, the penitentiary represents a reverse microcosm, a little world
in which self-dramatization counts for almost nothing. And in a world
view in which the complex and mysterious forces of circumstance press
in upon the individual actor, the penitentiary presents a world in which
the circumstances are utterly knowable and calculable: the sentence,
the building, the institutional rules. And all of this is done on a stage
of overwhelming physical presence, a century old, with a vast international reputation.

The penitentiary still stands and visitors still occasionally tour its

Figure 9. Cellblock 6, Eastern State Penitentiary, a photographic vision of the decaying
prison in 1993. Courtesy of the photographer, © Sandy Sorlien.

crumbling and evocative interior. There is, at least for now, no such thing as a last tour. There is also no such thing as a last interpretation. In the fall of 1993, the Eastern State Penitentiary Task Force of the Preservation Coalition of Greater Philadelphia organized an exhibition of photographs, displayed at Moore College of Art. The forty-eight images are astounding. The photographers manipulate texture and color, light and shade so that the prints have a dense abstract effect; with many of them it is not clear that one is seeing pictures of a decaying prison at all. Lit from above an empty cell takes on a mystical, visionary appearance. Shown closely, a wall of peeling paint looks like an expressionist manipulation of color and surface. It is an altogether original gathering of images; but in a sense the exhibit is a conventional thing to do, to take that great Rorschach of a building and superimpose upon it a fierce and relentless subjectivity.

5

Public Utility as Theme Park

Other destinations in Philadelphia were more credibly attractive through the mid-nineteenth century, more powerfully evocative, but none of them actually drew more visitors and moved them in such complex ways as the Fairmount Waterworks. Although the engineering of the water system had been evolving since 1801, the machinery of the waterworks, in the form it was to take in the years of its greatest distinction, was finished in 1822. The buildings of the Fairmount system were erected on the immediate grounds long revered as one of the country's great planned gardens. And in the two decades after 1822, the surrounding area was steadily improved into an extraordinarily varied parkland. The reputation of the complex as an essential place to see during the period far outranked the more obvious destinations, such as the great historical buildings. By the 1890s, however, the water system had long since ceased serving the entire city and Schuylkill River water was perceived, at least by nonnatives, as being undrinkable. Poor sanitation and drainage upstream had rendered the river at Fairmount odorous and uninviting. And the surroundings had lost their luster, both as a residential area and as pleasure grounds. And so it was only for something over a half century that the Fairmount Waterworks held such a place. But during that time, no other site in the city attracted visitors with such complicated enchantments. The simplest way of describing that contradictory magnetism is to say that, in the years of its greatest claim on the traveler, the Fairmount Waterworks was both a machine of a vastness and power not really comparable to anything else in the visitor's experience—and an idyll, a painter's dream, a happy world apart.

Caroline Gilman is a traveler of considerable charm although hardly to our taste now. Not ironic enough, not tart or suspicious, rarely uncomfortable, her sympathy and tenderness always central to any experience she re-creates, she is almost always happy to be where she is, happy to anticipate going to the next place, and happy to be there when she arrives. Still, her sensibility, if different from our own, can suggest why the waterworks was so fascinating in her time, the late 1830s.

Having drunk a glass of Schuylkill water chilled by Schuylkill ice, she visits the site, thinking of the river as God's spirit, spreading through "the dark channels of human life, seemingly lost until man inquires and strives for it," whereupon it pours forth its blessings on all who seek them, bringing health and joy. Aware that speaking of the beauty of the machinery will seem odd, she is determined to use the word anyhow. The machinery, she insists, *is* beautiful, its setting a perfect integration of God's abundance and the intelligence of man.

Had I been carried blindfold to the machinery at Fair Mount, and then permitted to behold it alone, I should have been agreeably excited by its singular combination of simplicity and power; its wheels would have rolled on a while in my memory, I should have paid the usual tribute of wonder to man's ingenuity, and have dreamt of those iron arms that seem so human in their operations; but now that I have gazed on the placid river, marked the shaded green of its beautiful borders, seen the sculptured images awaking graceful associations, stood by the clear basin and felt a longing like youth to rush in and stand under its showery fountain, heard the roar of the giant Art, contending with and counteracting the giant Nature, climbed the precipitous eminence, and watched the setting sun throwing his golden smile on all, this leaves a deeper stamp – the stamp of the beautiful.[1]

Even as she writes the passage, she holds a glass of cool water in her hand, tastes its freshness, and recalls the pleasures of having just seen what she now describes. Although she does not say so explicitly, it is clear that a potent satisfaction of the glass of water is that it has allowed her to be assimilated into the process she has just recounted. She has seen the river, the dam, the wheels and the pumps, the great standpipe and the beginnings of the distribution system, and now she receives the product, responds to it sensually, and ingests it, completing the cycle. Since she herself has given her description a religious resonance, it does not seem preposterous to think of her having converted something so uncomplicated and banal as drinking a glass of water into a kind of sacramental act, a secular eucharist.

As a sensory experience, seeing the Fairmount Waterworks, in Gilman's report of it, is multiple in the extreme. Still and placid, nonetheless the scene is full of sound and motion. Static and painterly, the experience is also highly kinetic: she is energized by being there and in order to see enough to satisfy her, she must walk, strenuously. There is even something tactile about being there, a response registered in skin and muscle: she is by no means the last visitor who imagines immersion in Schuylkill water, entering the pool, standing in the fountain. Of the mechanism itself, its arms and wheels are mechanical, metallic, and intimidating; yet they are, at the same time, anthropomorphic and humanoid. The waterworks' setting is vegetative, precipitous, and self-contained, Edenic, an extraordinary natural place; yet it is enhanced, not diminished, by the machinery in the foreground. The imagery evokes associations of the past—historical, mythic, divine—and pride in the present. God's majesty is inscribed in the scene, as is man's ingenuity.

Despite the aspect of Gilman's experience that seems pictorial, framed, situated, and static, one notices, as well, that it is plotted. Her description is a little narrative, extended through a portion of a day, in which she first sees the machinery, imagining what it would have been like to have seen it by approaching it blindfolded. She then observes, walks, and climbs. As the day ends, the excursion is over and the sun sets. Her quest, meanwhile, is resolved with the epiphanic realization that a rare and wonderful situation is actually possible, in the real world, in which industrial power, civic benefit, and the beauties of a remarkable place can coexist, reinforce each other, and not contend.

Contemporaneous with Gilman's travels, *Godey's Lady's Book* published a poem intended to accompany an engraving of the waterworks and its site. If Gilman's account tends to render the visit as an aesthetic experience, the poet Catherine L. Brooke takes that tendency a step farther. She first compares the sublimity of the view at Fairmount to famous places elsewhere. Although the Philadelphia view may be less high or deep or dramatic than other scenes, no other place surpasses its extraordinary play of light and shade and its ability to soothe the spirit. What really defines the aesthetic experience for the poet, however, is the contrast between the view of Fairmount and its valley in the middle distance and the view, through the distant haze, of "the crowded city"

> —where dwell
> Vice clothed in pomp, and suff'ring worth,
>   The dark of soul—the pure in heart—
> All that deform this glorious earth,
>   Or hope, or joy, to life impart,
> Are *struggling—living—dying* there;
>   And the heart sick'ning with the view,
> Gladly returns to Nature fair.[2]

Figure 10. A mid-nineteenth-century lithograph by Deroy of the Fairmount Waterworks, portraying it less as a mechanism for drawing water than as an embellishment of the pastoral scenery. Courtesy of the Library Company of Philadelphia.

The facile antiurbanism of the poet is not surprising: hating cities is a persistent strain in American cultural life from the mid-eighteenth century. What is simply astonishing is that it seems not to occur to the poet that the nature that serves as a refuge from the dark corruption of the distant city is a scene improved and arranged for fifty years in the interest of providing a site for a public utility and that "nature" is not a pristine river valley but a municipal water system. Determined to cast Fairmount as the happy valley, the antithesis to the unspeakable Philadelphia, she finds no difficulty in suppressing the relationship between the two.

Gilman's impressions, rendered in her lyrical prose, are striking, both for what they say and what they imply. And Brooke's verse is remarkable, not for the quality of her vision, certainly not for the craft of her verse, but for the sheer willfulness of her antithesis. Still, it is not altogether clear what Gilman and Brooke and a multitude of travelers like them actually saw when they visited the waterworks. What now exists is an odd complex of Greek Revival buildings, visible from the railroad and the highway, below the Art Museum, at river's edge, all in various stages of rehabilitation and decay. Walking the grounds, one finds a fountain here, a statue there, a walkway, a stone staircase, a partly reconstructed esplanade: haunting and intriguing, the elements do not reassemble themselves in the mind. No one could imagine now the relation between those buildings, the surroundings, and the municipal water supply of the middle third of the nineteenth century, nor could a person now imagine why anybody would have wished to visit the site.

One reason precedes and underlies any consideration of what was really there, at the site, and that is the absolute fascination of travelers from abroad with the use of water in America. For Mrs. Bromley, an English traveler in the 1860s, it was the consumption of water that left her astonished. "Immoderate water-drinkers," she calls Americans. "There is water in the trains, water in the boats, water in the railway stations, water in the drawing rooms." And, to make matters worse, with meals, Americans take either water or diluted milk.[3] To Captain Oldmixon, another English traveler in the fifties, startled by the ease with which hydrants were turned on, sending the water "rushing along the gutter in all directions," it is finally the use of water to extinguish fires—"a constant and vast consumption"—that most amazes him.[4] And to another English traveler, W. E. Baxter, it is the use of water in domestic life that seems so striking. Americans, he reports, "wash and scrub frequently, and all new erections have bath-rooms and other modern appliances necessary to health and comfort."[5] But it is the use of water on streets and steps that captivates travelers again and again, a passion for cleanliness that seems not so much national as uniquely Philadelphian. It is a "delightful virtue of neatness," writes Fanny Kemble, "carried almost to an inconvenience." From time to time, and especially early on Sunday morning, "the streets are really impassable, except to a good swimmer. 'Cleanliness,' says the old saw, 'is near to godliness.' Philadelphia must be very near heaven."[6] It is a subject on which Dickens must be allowed the last word. "Philadelphia," he writes, "is most bountifully provided with fresh water, which is showered and jerked about, and turned on, and poured off, everywhere."[7] For anyone interested in such a lavish use of water, and nearly all travelers were, the Fairmount Waterworks had a special magnetism.

As for attempting to recover a sense of what was there, it is immediately clear that the natural and the made, the scenic and the utilitarian coexisted and interpenetrated at every point. In the visitor's immediate foreground, the river widened to more than twice its normal width into a still basin, the result, of course, of an engineering decision to dam the river, collect a body of water, and ultimately divert a portion of the river through the buildings of the system. The result was the enhancement of a naturally lovely valley by extending the perspective. Across the basin lay a particularly varied and scenic shoreline. Looking past the dammed river to the east, one could see the spires and domes of the city. To the northwest, one could see the receding prospect of the river valley, its bridges, its wooded banks.

Boating on the Schuylkill at the time was extensive and picturesque, extending from small pleasure craft, to racing shells, to Durham boats, large working rowboats of the kind used by Washington to cross the Delaware, to stern-wheelers, which docked at Fairmount and shuttled tourists to East Falls, Laurel Hill Cemetery, and Manayunk. An advertisement in a contemporary guidebook describes the pleasures of these "Delightfully Romantic Schuylkill Excursions." They provide views of "handsome and interesting scenery," seven bridges crossing the Schuylkill and one over the Wissahickon Creek, four railroads, an inclined plane, a canal, and trains of over one hundred loaded cars.[8] As for the waters themselves, the indigenous rockfish, black bass, and catfish of the river had mixed with the golden carp, which had escaped from nearby ornamental gardens. And so fishermen could ordinarily be seen

Figure 11. Promenaders on the portico over the central building of the Fairmount Waterworks. The elegance of the dress is suggestive of the tone of the experience. Courtesy of Urban Archives, Temple University, Philadelphia.

in the foreground, from any perspective at Fairmount. One traveler, noting the fishermen with pleasure, will allude to Isaak Walton and another traveler will be reminded of the banks of the Seine. But seemingly all visitors were delighted to notice the fishermen, remember their presence, and think about them as an essential element in the composition.

During the half century of its greatest popularity, the area surrounding the Fairmount Waterworks was the single most impressive location for public art in the city. And a stroller of the grounds would rarely be out of sight of a piece of statuary. Opposite the building housing the great waterwheels, two fountains had been erected, one a marble basin containing a representation of a child astride a large fish, the mouth of the fish sending forth a stream of water of some eight or ten feet, the other a life-size figure by William Rush of a woman holding a water bird, generally known as "Nymph and Bittern," moved from the previous waterworks at Center Square. Two allegorical figures of monumental size, Justice and Wisdom, executed by William Rush in celebration of Lafayette's visit to the city in 1824, had been installed in the engine house. Two more of Rush's figures were placed on rocks above the forebay, with jets of water. Two other large figures by Rush, allegorical sculptures in wood representing the genius of the Schuylkill River, reclined over the entrances to the wheelhouses. Visitors seem not only to have appreciated the figures but to have entered into the spirit of the allegory, eagerly "reading" them. An interpretation of them was widely available during the midcentury decades; it pointed out that the bearded male is the Schuylkill, a chain attached to his wrist being emblematic of the river tamed by locks and dams, while a bald eagle at his feet "is about to abandon the banks of the Schuylkill in consequence of the busy scene which art is introducing." The female figure is seated near the pump; on her left side is a waterwheel and at her right elbow stands a large vase, representing the reservoir.[9]

Not far from the fountain stood a bust of Frederick Graff, the designer of the water system, in an intricate Gothic marble housing. Erected in 1848, it invariably caught the attention of travelers in midcentury, who were often quite moved by it. The bust seems to have personalized the experience, putting a human face on the great complex. And throughout its early years of development, a large number of incidental sculptures came to be placed here and there in the park. "The grounds," writes Lieutenant Colonel Maxwell, "are tastefully and beautifully arranged, with spouting Cupids, and all manner of other gods and goddesses."[10]

The buildings themselves gradually evolved from an engine house, containing the two steam engines that briefly drove the system prior to 1822, an old mill house, containing eight waterwheels, each sixteen feet in diameter, which provided the power to raise the water to the reservoir at the top of the hill after the demise of the steam engines, and two similarly neoclassical structures at each end, built at right angles, a caretaker's house and a Watering Committee building. From the start, they were designed in imitation of the great estates that occupied the hills above the river, suggestive, in their use of line and space, rather less of their industrial use than of the gracious living of the American aristocracy of the eighteenth century. Various ways were devised to accommodate visitors within the buildings. After 1835, the engine house was remodeled into a restaurant. But throughout the period from the twenties until late in the century, the principal view from within the buildings was of the working of the machinery from a balcony in the mill house. Every picture of the experience of the buildings and the gardens of the waterworks from that period makes it clear that being there was genteel and comfortable, leisurely and happy. But at the same time, being on the balcony over the great wheels was something like being in the belly of the beast. "The water is raised from the Schuylkill, to these reservoirs," writes Alfred Pairpoint, an English traveler of the mid-1850s,

by immense force-pumps, propelled by water-wheels of prodigious diameter, the very first sight and sound of which, as they suddenly roll round, distributing power by means of large cog-wheels to others of smaller size that work the pumps, are sufficient to bewilder and terrify the beholder. The place set apart for spectators to view the works is railed round and perfectly safe;—yet such is the vibration and din, that the strongest nerved persons are glad to make their exit after a brief inspection.[11]

Pairpoint's account suggests a correspondence with other experiences, in literature and life, of the sublime. The viewer is behind the rail, on the balcony, inside the fence. Beyond it are Miltonic extremes, of height and depth, light and dark, of precipitous movement, of noise, and most of all of danger. And the result is a frisson, an agreeable chill, comparable to a stylized and circumscribed view of the Alps, or the heights of Notre Dame, or Niagara Falls, or the great canyons of the American West; here, the great water machine of Philadelphia is awesome and frightening, but also safe and nonthreatening.

Besides the buildings, the machinery, the statuary, and the views, the grounds themselves provided an extraordinary range of experience, from the exquisitely planned South Garden to the specimen plantings of its middle areas to the natural woodlands and dramatic rock formations of its northern quadrant. Besides a number of small structures, an arbor here, a gazebo there, a summer house, an enclosed mineral spring, what the grounds presented was a constantly changing orientation. Approaching the main buildings from the solid ground of Fairmount itself, the visitor passed over the forebay, the dramatic inlet that carried a portion of the river through the pumping machinery, by means of a stone bridge. From that point on, visitors seem often to remember themselves as being situated differently, both in relation to the ground and the view, from moment to moment. They remember climbing, changing directions as they do so, and viewing with the changing panorama of 360

Figure 12. A view of the pleasure grounds adjacent to the Fairmount
Waterworks in 1875. Courtesy of Urban Archives, Temple University,
Philadelphia.

degrees, sometimes outside, exposed, above the river, sometimes inside, within the rocks and the vegetation. It is a contrast that illustrations of the experience emphasize, the sun-drenched view from the portico above the wheelhouse, the arches and tunnels and leaf canopies of the gardens, dark and slightly mysterious.

It is odd how rarely travelers use superlatives in describing the experience of visiting the waterworks. Even if they had not chosen to say so, it is hard to imagine that they did not know, at some level, that the complex embodied the biggest, the first, and the best. In an earlier stage, when the water was pumped by steam power, the high pressure engine devised for the purpose was the largest built up to that time. When the decision was made to employ the power of the river itself to drive the pumping machinery and a dam was built for that purpose, it was the largest dam in the world. The wheels of the pumping mechanism were the largest ever built and no system elsewhere raised anything comparable to the amount of water pumped at Fairmount. A fountain pressured by the water within the reservoir rose some forty or fifty feet, the highest fountain in the world. And no other city of consequence had engaged in a comparable civic project, to provide pure water to everyone within the urban limits, unfailingly, at reasonable cost.

Mrs. Trollope, notoriously, thought much of the United States tasteless, boring, and offensive when she toured it in 1827; she was indefatigable in comparing what she saw to European places, finding the American experience shallow, devoid of elegance and grace. Philadelphia, by and large, did not captivate her: it seemed monotonous and undramatic. But her visit to the waterworks did captivate her. She responds with a burst of lyrical prose in contrast to the generally acerbic tone of her book. Nothing in the passage suggests that she has read other people's accounts and indeed her visit occurs at the beginning of the period in which the waterworks was a major destination. Still, she encapsulates most of the strains of interest expressed through the mid-century by writers both before and after her visit.

She begins, as do many others, by cutting back and forth between the machinery ("vast, yet simple") and the setting ("one of the very prettiest spots the eye can look upon"). She draws the view, the great estate on the opposite shore, the weeping willows reflected, the dam, producing "the sound and look of a cascade," the buildings, the terrace, the rock wall, the stream of water, "clear and bright as crystal," received in a basin with a cup nearby for the thirsty traveler.

At another point, a portion of the water in its upward way to the reservoir is permitted to spring forth in a perpetual *jet-d'eau*, that returns in a silver shower upon the head of a marble *naiad* of snowy whiteness. The statue is not the work of Phidias, but its dark, rocky background, the flowery catalpas which shadow it, and the bright shower through which it shows itself, altogether makes the scene one of singular beauty; add to which, the evening on which I saw it was very sultry, and the contrast of this cool spot to all beside certainly enhanced its attractions; it was impossible not to envy the nymph her eternal shower-bath.[12]

One realizes with a startled surprise that the formidable Mrs. Trollope, like Caroline Gilman, has imagined the pleasures of standing in the fountain.

Consider, from Mrs. Trollope's description, what came together in her experience of the waterworks: a genuinely sublime scene in which elements that gave the scene its sublimity—the river, the cliff, the hill—were enlisted in the service of technology; real machines so large, so potent, so awesomely designed as to seem sublime themselves; the movement of enough water up a hill to serve a city of a half million; and a statue of a classical goddess taking a perpetual shower at the base of the cliff. Ever alert to the possibility of bad taste in America, Mrs. Trollope is unfazed by that particular blend of good taste, no taste, and bad taste. More than its mixture of taste, the scene holds together in some kind of amazing equipoise a powerful reality—real river, real pump, real reservoir—along with what Umberto Eco calls "hyperreality": a Victorian rendering of a Greek deity standing in a stream of water devised to look like a natural fountain. It was a combination waterworks and theme park. And the mythic charge was so heavy and complex that it offered more visual, tangible satisfaction, more cultural validation, than the more plausible destinations, such as the State House, could ever have offered.

Aspects of Mrs. Trollope's description that echo a taste for a Victorian, domesticated sublime are easy enough to understand. Curiously, her fondness for the machinery is just as characteristic of her period as her attraction to blossoms and waterfalls. It is a taste that John Sears calls "the industrial sublime." People in the nineteenth century loved machines, were awed and moved by them; the culmination of that taste occurred, for Americans, with the Centennial Exposition in Philadelphia in 1876, a large portion of which was given to the display of machinery. Even the descriptions of certain natural wonders draws upon the diction of technology in a way that no one at the time found contradictory. Sears writes, of tourists in the American West: "The landscape

of the Yellowstone geyser basins both looked and sounded like a factory. The Upper Geyser Basin 'suggested to my modern mind a manufacturing center in full swing,' wrote Owen Wister. 'It might have been
Lowell.'" [13]

Clearly, the capacity to see a machine as an aesthetic object deserving of awe and the ability to use that valuation so as to totalize and orga-
nize the world were assumptions carried to the Fairmount Waterworks
by most of its visitors, although such assumptions were rarely acknowledged or intellectualized. They are clearer now than they were at the
time. Other motives also lie nearly buried in the accounts of the waterworks, needing the distance of a century to surface. And one of them is
signaled by a remarkable shift in the mode of description when the traveler, approaching Fairmount, renders in words what he has seen.

Consider the curiously titled *American Photographs* by Jane and
Marion Turnbull. Without illustrations, the book is photographic only in
a metaphorical sense. Not so opinionated as some nor so lyrical as others, it is a series of impressions of the United States at the end of the
1850s in which the visual is obviously meant to predominate. Written
with grace and style and an eye for the telling detail, it is, for all that, not
terribly different from dozens of other accounts of the United States by
Europeans at midcentury.

Visiting Philadelphia, the Turnbulls waste no time in seeking out
the waterworks. It is, they report, "about two miles from the city," constructed on an area of thirty acres, at "an expense of 450,000 dollars."
Fairmount itself is situated "100 feet above tide water in the river below,
and about sixty feet above the most elevated ground in the city." There
are four reservoirs "capable of containing 22,000,000 gallons. The area
of the reservoirs is six acres; they are twelve feet deep and lined with
stone. The dam is 1600 feet long, the race 400 feet long, 90 feet wide. The
Mill House is made of stone and it is 238 feet long, 56 feet wide. And the
pumps raise 1,250,000 gallons of water every twenty-four hours." [14]

The waterworks episode in the Turnbulls' account of it is not without its charm, its personal engagement, its eye for the happy detail. But
those aspects are completely outweighed by the obsessive, almost numbing facticity of the passage. One looks elsewhere in the book to see if that
dimension is always there. It is not. The Turnbulls do not approach their
destinations with tape measure in hand. Visiting New York City, they reveal the dimensions of Trinity Church in lower Manhattan and the extent of the Croton Aqueduct. But facts and figures, on their visit to New

York, are rare. A little later, they visit Niagara, where they are properly awed. But the height of the falls, the breadth, the estimated volume of water, the number of visitors, none of these engage them. Elsewhere they visit the full range of cities from Boston to New Orleans and nothing of their obsession with quantity and measurement appears. In Philadelphia, only Girard College engages a similar interest. But that is another story.

Lest the mode of description of the Turnbulls seem unique to them, consider a different traveler, contemporaneous and English though not at all alike in sensibility, less lyrical than they, rather more interested in the institutional life of the Republic. The dam across the Schuylkill, writes Charles Richard Weld, is sixteen hundred feet long. "Powerful hydraulic machinery is set in motion, which raises 8000 gallons of water per minute to reservoirs 100 feet high, occupying an area of six acres."[15]

The relentless facticity of those passages is not rhetorical, done to impress or move the reader. The Turnbulls knew perfectly well that a reservoir that holds twenty-two million gallons is not necessarily any more impressive, as a statistic offered up to the willing reader, than a reservoir that holds seventeen million gallons, or, for that matter, a reservoir described with words only and not numbers. The facts are there because they serve some need of the writers themselves.

That mode of description, which seems so positivistic, so given to quantity and measurement, may appear, at first, rather bloodless, a retreat from feeling. It is, of course, quite the opposite. The facts and the numbers are the recourse of writers struck with wonder, knowing that conventional descriptive prose, in the face of a technological spectacle so immense, will simply not convey the magnitude of the subject. Wonder with a touch of pathos. The travelers themselves do not need to name its source. The sensibility out of which that response comes is written in the literature of the city for two centuries.

Simmel's "The Metropolis and Mental Life" is still the defining conceptualization of urban psychology. In the small group, Simmel writes, "production serves the customer who orders the good, so that the producer and the consumer are acquainted." In the modern metropolis, on the other hand, goods are produced for "the market, that is, for entirely unknown purchasers who never personally enter the producer's actual field of vision." From such a depersonalized economy, certain common traits of mind and temperament follow: a punctuality and exactness, for example, a blunting of discrimination, an aggressive energy, and it is these qualities of distance and ultimately of loneliness that occupy Simmel as his essay opens outward.[16] Simmel's perceptions were not unique to him or altogether original; readers of Dickens and Gogol, Melville and Poe are perfectly aware of just those anomic qualities of urban life. Life, in cities, is lived among strangers and many of the most vital processes of life are conducted out of sight and out of mind.

It is not all bad, that urban distance and anonymity. Considering the rural and small-town residents of Wisconsin in 1890, the burdens of labor there, and its psychological toll, Michael Lesy casts a very different light on the life of the city. "Those strangers, those anonymities, could slaughter animals in a secret place, butcher them, prepare them, cook them, and serve them, all for a small sum of money which, once presented, obligated the bearer to nothing more than the satisfaction of his appetite."[17] Those strangers could entertain and inform and cure disease. And the fact that one did not know them was a small price to pay for the comparative ease of city life.

And so there was, first, the wonder of the water itself, inexhaustible and pure, supplied everywhere within the limits of the city, with pressure sufficient to reach a fourth story. There was, second, the fact that all of this was done by pipes and mechanisms underground and out of sight, engineered and controlled by men one could not know or would not have any reason to wish to. But third, there was the fact that one could *see* the system and understand its principles. It was a situation that allowed the pleasure Lesy writes of–not having to find water, or pump it, or carry it, or concern oneself with its purity or its amount, or enlist the help of someone to bring it, rather having it supplied by strangers, the water to be summoned by the turning of a tap. At the same time, it was a situation that allowed a single person to break through that dull distance that Simmel writes of and scores of writers of fiction have evoked. All of those facts and figures used by the travelers represent small personal triumphs of intimacy and comprehension, all of the distance and anonymity of urban life held at bay for a moment. There are, perhaps, no more instances after the demise of the Fairmount Waterworks, of a facility so large and so important that is, at the same time, so comfortably accessible and so intelligible, so graspable to the layperson.

6

Urban Woods

From time to time an observant and whimsical writer will publish a book on the natural history of Manhattan. Although the idea has generated several such books by now, they continue to be written and they continue to find readers. The idea has such allure not only because there really is a great variety of natural life in New York City. Such works get read because the idea is captivating. It cuts across the grain: songbirds over the financial district, wildflowers just off Seventh Avenue. The norm is, of course, otherwise. The great visions of New York written by people who do not live there confront its urban density head-on, trying to lever up the secrets of the city, savoring its complexities and contradictions, embracing its concrete and glass, leaving birds and flowers to the country travelers. As for picturesque vistas within the limits of New York, the contour of the land in the city has long since either been obliterated or rendered unnoticeable (always excepting Central Park) and the views a traveler would now record are bridges and buildings, streets and people, the signs and portents of urban life, not hills and valleys.

A moment's reflection persuades us that aspects of experience that seem to us urban and aspects that seem rural overlap and interpenetrate at every point. But we have come, through the habits of two hundred years, indeed two thousand years, to exaggerate the gulf between city and country, to express ourselves as if these were polar extremities and discrete worlds. Although writers on the spirit of place may be remarkably virtuose, the sensibilities of most writers do, of course, tend to be split, one side or the other, firmly urban or firmly rural.

The polarity was somewhat different in the nineteenth century. For one thing, it was far more likely than it has been in our time to embrace within the same book observations on cities and observations on the rural spaces between them. Even if a traveler wished primarily to visit cities, it took a long time to get from one to another and most travelers liked to respond to the passing countryside. More than the massive thereness of American spaces, the scenery of the continent beckoned to the traveler before the fact as a series of highly charged tableaux. Depending on one's frame of reference, perhaps fifty famous places, perhaps two hundred fifty, defined what the United States looked like. And engravings and lithographs–of the Delaware Water Gap, for example, or Old Faithful Geyser–appeared throughout the publications of the century.

Such views had evolved as a body of more-or-less official natural scenery because they seemed to define an especially American majesty and drama. Such a large series of specific views, framed and set apart, infinitely reproduced, evoked the power of the American landscape to move the spectator by a particularly American kind of sublimity. And so it was to such places as Niagara Falls and Yosemite, the White Mountains and the Hudson Valley, Mammoth Cave and a dozen harbor views such as Charleston and Baltimore that nineteenth-century travelers came as eagerly as they came to the cities of the new republic. Having carried the famous views in the mind from seeing them in not one magazine but several, travelers sought to enter the frame, recovering that rectangular view of the sacred place and actually, physically, stepping into it.

Even if nineteenth-century travelers could include the urban and the rural in a single book and even if they pursued the great views of the North American continent with a fluid catholicity, it is still true, nevertheless, that the two worlds, the rural and the urban, were seen as being antithetical. Nineteenth-century travelers were often fascinated by the abruptness with which the edge of the city meets something resembling wilderness, an observation confirming the gap between the city and the not-city. For a very long time, the purpose of travel has been either natural scenery or cities and people. When the two coexist in a single sensibility, it is likely to seem so odd as to appear evidence of either a remarkable virtuosity or a special act of will.

Philadelphia, as always, is a little different from anywhere else and the rules that seem to govern the observation of the United States at large break down in the face of a city bearing its age and showing a development not like other cities. For a very long time, it has been the gracious urbanity of the city that travelers expect to find, its institutions and its buildings, its poise and reserve. That is what travelers have been told that they will find in Philadelphia. And that is indeed what they do find, with very little sense of mystery and surprise. In one way, however, the visual aspect of Philadelphia *is* often surprising, a way that has, precisely, to do with city, country, and the difference between them.

Figure 13. A mid-nineteenth-century engraving by Rawdon, Wright, and Hatch of an outing on the Wissahickon Creek, in which the inhabitants of the city encounter the wilderness. Courtesy of the Library Company of Philadelphia.

More than patches of parkland, the visitor gradually comes to realize, Philadelphia contains, within its limits, areas of forest, hills and valleys, birds and beasts, pristine streams, distant views and prospects. Throughout the nineteenth century and well into the twentieth, Philadelphia presents a fusion of urban life and natural landscape, it integrates urban picturesque and rural picturesque, and it dramatizes a unique interpenetration of the "natural" and spontaneous into the rationalized and systematized life of the metropolis. No other city in the United States and perhaps anywhere presents an implicit aesthetics of place that is comparable. An apparently hyperbolic but really rather official view of the late nineteenth century maintains that

There is no city where the varieties of wild landscape so closely surround and so boldly invade a civilization given over to material industries. Besides the broad Delaware, the exquisite Schuylkill, a stream far more beautiful than the Arno, bathes one side of the city, and into this Italian sheet of water slides the wild Wissahickon, coming down pure from its "savage gorges and cold springs" as primitive as a stream of the wilderness, yet easily accessible to the most sedentary citizen. The conditions of climate, which blend at this particular spot the characters of the arctic and semi-tropical regions, combining the summer southern fruits, birds, and insects, with the sports of northern snow and ice, add peculiar variety to its artistic aspects.[1]

Philadelphia as the best of both worlds, the best of many worlds: it is a view, however eccentric now, that would not have seemed odd in the late nineteenth century.

Among those writers struck, often implicitly, with the interpenetration of the country into the urban spaces of Philadelphia, consider first an English traveler named, appropriately or ironically for the present context, Finch—precisely, I. Finch. Arriving in Philadelphia in the 1830s he set down some of the more conventional observations of the time, without much color or enthusiasm. "There are some manufacturing establishments in Philadelphia," he reports, "and several thousand looms are employed." Soon into his description of the city, however, he reveals a purpose for being in Philadelphia that transcends the general curiosity of the nineteenth-century traveler. He wishes to search out and honor the tomb of Wilson the ornithologist. (Although his context fills in a few details of the indomitable Wilson, it does not really identify him; Finch quite obviously assumes that anyone curious enough and cultured enough to read *him* would also know, without prompting, who Wilson was.) Having found the tomb of Alexander Wilson in the graveyard of the early Swedish church Gloria Dei, Finch pays his tribute: "While the birds continue to frequent the woods of America, so long will the lovers of nature admire the ornithology of Wilson, and every naturalist who goes to the city of peace should pay a visit to his tomb." Finch reads the epitaph and adds, "He desired to be buried where the birds might sing over him, and his desire has been complied with."[2]

No conclusions, perhaps, should be drawn from the sweet and touching devotion of Finch to the ornithologist. Some conclusions can be drawn, however, from the way in which Finch "reads" Philadelphia. The Swedish cemetery is easily identified; it is still there. It is and was within sight of the waterfront, a five-minute walk from the major docks of the city, off to the side a bit but still within the metropolitan center. It is transformed, in Finch's view, into something resembling the cemetery of an English country parish. Birds sing over Wilson's grave and Philadelphia is "the city of peace."

Charles Augustus Murray, also traveling in the thirties, gives a different but related version of Philadelphia as a special place, without a boundary, the forest coexisting with the city.

The morning was bright as a young May sun could make it; the Schuylkill wound gracefully round the base of the eminence on which I stood, his banks fringed with the oak, the poplar, and the weeping willow, and studded with many white and smiling villas . . . , while, stretched on the seaward plain, lay the peaceful city of Brotherly Love, its bright spires glittering above the light hazy smoke. . . . No pen can describe the beauty of the forest-foliage at this 'sweet hour of prime;' so great was the variety of tree and shrub which clothed the undulating hills around, all spangled with early dew, the brilliant dog-wood shining through every casual opening and the lap of earth beneath teeming with the honeysuckle, the azalea, the wild fusia, and hundreds of humbler, though not less lively, flowrets.[3]

It is rather like those photographs of vegetation, in the tradition of Eliot Porter, that reproduce distant configurations with perfect clarity while also reproducing every leaf and every fold of bark in the foreground. What one needs to remember, because it is so lightly mentioned, is that in the middle distance of this Eden, this botanist's paradise, stands the city of Philadelphia. Murray's view shares nothing with the pilgrimage of Finch except for one thing: the common tendency to see Philadelphia as a blessed place, remarkable for its ability to contain and nurture the energies of the natural world.

James Dixon, visiting the city a few years later, enters into his description of Philadelphia with a comparable emphasis, although with an intent that is broader, even more enthusiastic, quite explicitly mythic. Dixon turns out, in the long run, not to like Philadelphia very much. But he opens the subject of the city with an ecstatic tribute to the union of the natural and the man-made that is extraordinary. Approaching the city from the river, he sees it rise before him, "peering towards the skies as bright as those of Italy, resting on the bosom of a country as fertile as imagination can conceive." The river is the site of commerce and of sweeping natural beauty. And the location of the city is, quite simply, perfect.

The assemblage of favourable circumstances seems complete. Earth and sky, land and water, all combine to produce the effect. Nature has certainly selected this spot as for the purpose of showing, in the beauties of even a ruined world, some faint outline, some faded image, of what Paradise must have been.[4]

Despite the ecstatic vision of a perfect Philadelphia, Dixon does find the grid plan wearisome and the streets too uniform. But his sense of the union of the natural world and the city of man is in no way undermined by his later weariness with the same city. The first vision is mythic, the city as earthly paradise, the second is quotidian, the city as the site of a large amount of predictable business, all carried out in an area resembling a checkerboard, and the two visions stand in a kind of parallel validity.

A few years after Dixon's tour, Thoreau chanced to pass through Philadelphia. He visited the State House and was pleased by the view from the cupola. But what engaged him most was the wildlife, not only its species but its immediacy. "Was interested in the squirrels, gray and black, in Independence and Washington Squares. Heard they have, or have had, deer in Logan Square."[5] Making every allowance for the oddity of Thoreau's angle of vision, his pleasure and surprise do not seem, really, very odd, as he discovers, with interest, that wildlife coexists in one of the most densely concentrated centers of human activity, the second largest in the country. It is a discovery that would surprise and delight anyone. With the discovery of the wildlife in the city goes the corollary, implicitly, following from the very note of surprise and delight, that such a rich and dramatic coexistence of the natural and the urban is very far from being the case in all cities.

When travel narratives in the decades of mid-nineteenth century touch on the striking presence of the life of nature within the metropolitan limits of Philadelphia, they almost invariably include one of three elements, sometimes all three. The first is a mythic aspect. Nature in Philadelphia seems somehow legendary, out of history, elemental, with a hint of the prelapsarian perhaps, or a suggestion of Penn's founding intention to make a "greene country town." Even if none of those nineteenth-century travelers had known of the vision of the primitive painter Edward Hicks, his tendency to devise ever new versions of the Peaceable Kingdom and entwine them with the arrival of William Penn did not simply derive from his own gentle imagination or the Quaker circles in which he moved. It was a broader current of assent that had selected Philadelphia as one of the benign places on the earth. Nineteenth-century travelers, by and large, love Baltimore, for example, but no one thinks of Baltimore as having, within its boundaries, remarkable and dramatic birds and beasts along with elements of a pristine landscape.

Many of the strands of that mythic charge that envelopes the idea of the city are elusive, and ineffable. But some of them are quite concrete. Lady Hardy, traveling in the late nineteenth century, observes that much of the parkland within the city was not "made"; rather it was organized around "primeval forest trees, rocky mounds, and sparkling rivers of the dead ages."[6] The perception that the city contains, inscribed within its official recreational areas, compelling evidence of its antique, prehistoric past is a startling one, which invites a reading of the city as an enactment of something legendary and archetypal.

The second aspect of such references is a quite deliberate and self-conscious pictorialism. Surely travel writing in all times and places has a strong visual element. But there is a difference between wishing the reader to know what a given place looks like and wishing the reader to see a picture of it. Consider Charles Augustus Murray's lyric passage above. He establishes the nature and the direction of the light. Then he establishes his own position as viewer, inviting the reader to share his perspective. Then he fills in the middle distance with some general and casual strokes: "many white and smiling villas." And finally he evokes the sheer plenitude of the nearby vegetation in an especially diagrammatic way: "the brilliant dogwood shining through every casual opening." Murray does not really wish the reader to see what he sees. He wishes the reader to see an imagined painting of what he sees.

Or in James Dixon's arrangement, "Earth and sky, land and water, all combine to produce the effect," summarizing his framed and centered vision of the city. The reader is encouraged to assist in filling in the picture, putting the light and the clouds in the sky, the color and the vegetation in the earth, the city on the shore, meeting the water in the foreground, the sky at the top of the painting, a "faded image," perhaps, of the city of God but a bright and compelling image of the city of the present.

The third aspect of such commentary is its tendency to remove anything human from the visual description. When travelers try to capture their sense of the pleasures of nature within Philadelphia, nobody walks or sits, by and large, within their verbal scenery, nobody rows a boat or rides a horse, certainly no one speaks or enacts any kind of social role. In prints of the period, in contrast with those verbal accounts of Philadelphia's scenic places, something like the classic pastoral arrangement of the picturesque and the human usually does appear. Within the center of the design, a few people appear, in rather static and stagy postures suggestive of bucolic life. In Augustus Koellner's depiction of the waterworks, lithographed by Deroy and published between 1849 and 1851, for example, the vegetation of the nearer shore occupies the bottom fourth of the image, the sky the upper half, with the middle portion including the river, the farther shore, the waterworks, and an extraordinary number of human figures, ranging from a young man and his dog in the foreground, to over a score of tiny people in the stern-wheeler in mid-picture, to an extraordinary number of figures in the far distance, at the promenade, in the small boats, even crossing the wire bridge. All of them seem to be happily at leisure. The print would be diminished without its human figures, so emblematic are they of the quiet pleasures to be found within such a scene: they enable the viewer to enter the scene and imagine floating within it, walking, riding the steamboat. The contrast with the prose descriptions of the traveling writers is remarkable. It is not clear whether they are so struck with their comparative ability to escape from people while still being within the city that a desocialized element overtakes their natural scenery or whether, for some other reason lost in the implicit aesthetics of the time, human figures are irrelevant to their vision of the quiet and sacred places within the city. In any case, those verbal renderings of wild nature within Philadelphia are as emptied of other people as the scenes on a calendar.

I have spoken of the limited number of endlessly reproduced views of great American scenes. For a time in the later half of the nineteenth century, the country had something resembling a pictorial canon, a collection of scenic places, which would often appear with an accompanying description, justifying their power to move the instructed and sympathetic viewer, the engravings establishing the most visited or most "official" or most picturesque versions of the scenic place, its appropriate framing, distance, and relationship to the viewer's line of sight. There is nothing new, of course, in scenic views of American places at that time. William Birch's comprehensive and quite wonderful *City of Philadelphia* appeared, as a completed set, in 1800, followed by Cephas G. Childs's *Views of Philadelphia* in 1827 to 1830. What *was* new by the 1860s was the possibility of an American series, containing views from the whole country, establishing a national version of American picturesque.

Precisely such a collection was William Cullen Bryant's two-volume folio work called *Picturesque America*, published in 1872, consisting of essays by various hands and a large number of scenic engravings. If "coffee-table book" had been a phrase current in the seventies, it would have been the supreme coffee-table book of its decade. All of the views are enchanting, in the way that engravings of the period can be to the twentieth-century eye; perhaps more enchanting are the ones that, unintentionally, carry a nostalgic culture shock for us now: our own blighted cities such as Detroit or Newark shown as idyllic harbor towns.

Thinking about the nineteenth century's sense of the picturesque, it is clear how artificial it would be to try to divide the views of Bryant's book into those that are primarily urban and those that are rural. Even the views that are wholly urban have about them a charm that is wholly devoid of the rough-and-tumble energy of the Hogarth-Rowlandson-Cruikshank tradition. Cities are very pretty in Bryant's book, elements in a composition including, often, water and boats, trees and sky. Still, there is something different about the views of Philadelphia in collections such as Bryant's and it is this: pictures of Philadelphia in the last half of the nineteenth century customarily include several that seem to be *totally* rural, views without commerce or any sense of routine activity, with few if any people in them. Views of Fairmount Park and the Wissahickon Valley appear this way. And the striking fact about them is that the places portrayed lie within the city limits.

The Wissahickon Valley, in fact, took on an enormous iconic significance in those middle decades of the nineteenth century. The creek and its setting had long been a legendary place for residents of Philadelphia, more told about than visited. But in 1822 a substantial amount of rock was cut away to facilitate access to the creek. And the visitors began to arrive: ordinary travelers, amateur geologists, painters and sketchers, famous writers, and, the most enchanting of them all, an actress.

Fanny Kemble's diaries of her observations while on an acting tour with her father, the actor, are still quite readable for their art and grace. She has an actor's eye for the nuances of self-presentation and a painter's eye for color and shade. Independent and irreverent, she is also capable of a kind of naive wonder. Her visit to the Wissahickon Valley does not bulk large in her descriptions of the eastern states. But it became known at once that Fanny Kemble had been deeply impressed by the area. And her endorsement of its scenic power has served as a touchstone ever since.

It was a late December day in 1832 when she visited the Wissahickon; the light was soft and bright and the day seemed dreamlike. There were icicles in fantastic patterns but the creek was not frozen and it fell over the dam "like a curtain of gold," reflecting the red sun in "splinters of light." Like so many others, she organizes her observations

Figure 14. A characteristic portrayal of the Wissahickon Creek,
wild but not intimidating, here in summer. The human figures
almost blend into the natural formations. Courtesy of Urban
Archives, Temple University, Philadelphia.

into an imagined painting, the brook in the center flanked by tufted ce-
dars, the mill and its pond in the middle distance, "a most enchanting
and serene subject of contemplation."[7]

In the century following, the responses to the scenery of the creek
and its surroundings are extraordinary for their breadth and quality. In

Figure 15. Always, the idea of the Wissahickon Creek
carries the implicit understanding that just beyond where
one happens to be, there is a place of rocks and water, trees
and sunlight—and no people. Courtesy of Urban Archives,
Temple University, Philadelphia.

late 1993, the Library Company of Philadelphia organized an exhibition
of the portrayals of the Wissahickon Creek. It included maps and guidebooks, oils, watercolors, engravings, drawings, photographs, a panel of
needlepoint, postcards, stereographs, the romantic tales of George Lippard, a prose sketch by Poe.[8] Perhaps it is Christopher Morley, writing in
the twenties, who best brackets the nearer end of the vogue of the creek.
When his mother was a small girl in England, he writes, there stood, in
her father's house, a silk lampshade containing painted versions of the
world's scenic wonders.

There were vistas of Swiss mountains, Italian lakes, French cathedrals, Dutch
canals, English gardens. And then, among these fabled glories, there was a tiny
sketch of a scene that chiefly touched my mother's girlish fancy. She did not ever
expect to see it, but often, as the evening lamplight shone through it, her eye
would examine its dainty charm. It was called "The Wissahickon Drive, Philadelphia, U.S.A."[9]

The pleasures of nature within the limits of Philadelphia might all
have changed by the end of the nineteenth century. The city had worn
more than it had regenerated. And large areas of the city had become, depending on one's view, either extraordinary centers for skilled artisans
within the industrial process, or, changing one's angle of vision, one vast
sweatshop. It was always a little eccentric to notice the islands of sweet
nature within the metropolis of Philadelphia. By the turn of the century, it
might have seemed perverse. But it is a way of seeing the city that does not
die then, does not ever die really, and continues to the present time.

Two turn-of-the-century visitors confirm the continuity of an idyllic
version of Philadelphia. Lafcadio Hearn, writing to a friend, responds to
her mention of Philadelphia in a previous letter. "Oh!–you spoke about
Philadelphia. . . . Is it possible you have never seen it? Is it possible you
have never seen Fairmount Park?" It is, he thinks, "the most beautiful
place of the whole civilized world on any sunny, tepid summer day,"
Central Park being "a cabbage-garden by comparison." Its size is immense, its woods and terraces and knolls beautiful, its vistas breathtak-
ing. Often one is alone; but even if there are people, thousands of them,
the park absorbs them in sheltered spaces where they can scarcely be
seen. On a warm day, carriages pass, each with a pair of lovers.

Everybody in the park seems to be making love to somebody. Love is so much
the atmosphere of the place,–a part of the light and calm and perfume–that you
feel as if drenched with it, permeated by it, mesmerized.[10]

A few years later, Jacques Offenbach visited the city on a tour, conducting his own music. With an idle Sunday, he is advised to go to Indian Rock in Fairmount Park. It takes two hours to get there, he notes, "but you never leave the park." Philadelphians are justly proud of their "immense garden." And indeed they should be, "for it is most beautiful and picturesque—here and there tiny houses half-hidden by the thickets, streams winding beneath the trees, cool valleys, shady ravines, superb trees, thick woods." Offenbach ends the passage with a bright and vivid vignette, involving a café, some drunken coachmen, and two splendidly efficient policemen. But the moment is dominated by his uncommon admiration for a place of such pristine and bucolic beauty, so extensive, and within the city.[11]

In 1925, the *Century* published an essay by Samuel Scoville Jr. called "The Wildness of Philadelphia: How Nature Persists in a Metropolis." The title gives it away, of course. Whether Scoville knows it or not, he is working in an area of the imagination that is commonplace almost from the time at which Philadelphia emerged as a major North American metropolis. Coming down from the fragrant hills of Connecticut, Scoville finds only heat, noise, and dust in Philadelphia. But into the night, over the endless sounds of the trolley cars, Scoville hears the cry of the nighthawk, a sound heavily suggestive, for him, of his rural childhood.

That sweltering night in the city I felt as if the bird had come down from the north country as a special messenger to tell me that the way was still open and the peace still waiting—and I fell asleep to dream of green pastures and cool hilltops.[12]

Nighthawks actually live in cities now, he muses, nesting on the roofs of apartment buildings, camouflaging their eggs against the pebbled surface of the flat roofs, hunting by streetlight. And few, in fact, can be found in the country any more. As he moves on, he suggests his ease with the sound of the birds by miming them in print: "Whit, whit, whit," or "Whee-udel, whee-udel, whee-udel, whee-udel," or "Peto, peto." And the point of it all is that these lovely and comfortable sounds can be heard by anyone who will listen, well within the western limits of Philadelphia, specifically around Forty-seventh Street.

It is a charming essay, lyric and personal, a theme and variations. Once set in motion, this is the format of the variations. They establish the writer's presence at a place precisely identified with its urban location, he being alone within the scene, thoroughly familiar with the city, willing to be surprised. With a few strokes, they demonstrate the apparent hostility of the location to birds and trees, wild fungi, butterflies. And then, with a touching intimacy, the natural object is brought into focus, existing nonproblematically amid the brick and cement, the smoke and noise. In the center of the city, bobolinks pass by on their way south and blackpoll warblers call "Tseep, tseep" as they fly to Brazil. There are the edible mushrooms in a patch of grass near City Hall and the bald cypress growing incongruously amid the office towers. And to cap the series, one March day, a mourning cloak butterfly enters his open office window at Thirteenth and Locust Streets, as if to tell him that spring has come to the meadows and woods beyond the city.

In the years since, most of the wonder has eroded from the visitor's view of the natural places within the city and the natural life that thrives there. For one thing, many of the places have declined in the quality of experience they seem to offer: too many people, not enough will or imagination or public funds to maintain them. For another, they seem inevitably less separate, less Edenic, than they would have seemed a few years ago. Norman Mailer has remarked that it is impossible now to be out of the sound of a motor. If it seems to be so, even in the truly wild places of the earth, how much it must seem to be the case in a segment of Fairmount Park, let us say, that embraces the Schuylkill River and contains a view not much different from one of Eakins's paintings of scullers on the river, but which also contains, out of sight perhaps but not out of hearing, the major East Coast rail corridor, some ten lanes of high speed automobile traffic, dozens of lesser streets, overhead air traffic, and all of the small motors of daily life. No longer separate aurally, those vibrant natural places are not separate visually; they bear the wrappers and cans, the trampled vegetation, that speak to their absorption into the life of the city; not vast areas of Paradise any more, miraculously preserved against encroachment, within the metropolis, rather parks instead, natural perhaps but used, meant to be used. Earlier visitors to the natural places of the city sometimes posed themselves alone, as if "discovering" the Wissahickon Valley. No one would imagine such an encounter now. The natural places are perfectly familiar. More than the neutralization of those Edenic places, the myth that energizes it becomes hollow and obsolete. Thirty years after its publication, Leo Marx's *The Machine in the Garden* still names the myth, describes its nature and its energy, and marks its demise, the existence of technopolitan, machine-age culture in a setting capable of being seen as virginal and prelapsarian. The Edenic places in Philadelphia, the vitality of its wildlife, the magic of its scenery, these are connected in the most obvious way to the larger myth of America as the fulfillment of a pastoral ideal. And the myth loses its potency precisely as the machine conquers the garden, technology diminishing the possibility of imagining American destiny as being fulfilled through the landscape of the garden. All of which is to say that, even if, by some miracle, those pristine places of Philadelphia had remained as sheltered and vibrant as they once were, they would still not be able to generate the same kind of epiphanic joy in the observer that they once did, their mythic underpinnings being, by now, dispelled.

Still, an echo of that older response is not impossible. Early in Bill Bryson's *The Lost Continent: Travels in Small-Town America*, he drives northward, through the megalopolitan eastern seaboard. And in due course he arrives in Philadelphia. He reflects on the civic administration of the city with benign amusement, turning over in his mind some of the more recent instances of municipal corruption. And he visits Independence Hall, offering his respect but declining to stand in the unmoving line in order to get inside. Meeting some old friends and beginning to drive to their home in the northwestern part of the city, he is suddenly overtaken by the single unequivocally positive observation he has to make on Philadelphia and the people who live there.

The road to Mount Airy led through the most beautiful city park I had ever been in. Called Fairmount Park and covering almost 9,000 acres, it is the largest municipal park in America and it is full of trees and flowering shrubs and bosky glades of infinite charm. It stretches for miles along the banks of the Schuylkill River. We drove through a dreamy twilight. Boats sculled along the water. It was perfection.[13]

The passage would be less striking were it not for the determination of Bryson not to be taken in by all that is bogus and bloated in American life, the kitsch and the pseudoauthenticity. It is as if he is ambushed by an American place that is not inflated but is huge, not promoted but perfectly beautiful. And the passage is as striking as it is because we know what he could not have known when he wrote it: that he is one of the more recent observers in a sequence two centuries old of travelers who have found a special joy in the wild places within the city.

7

American Athens

The anonymous author of *Things as They Are; or, Notes of a Traveller*, writing in 1834, muses over the phrase "the Athens of America." "Why Philadelphia should not be the Athens of America," he writes, "I am sure I cannot tell, nor what should prevent Baltimore, Boston, or New York. The people have all the means within their reach."[1] And another mid-nineteenth-century traveler writes that "Philadelphia resembles Edinburgh in several particulars. They have both assumed to themselves, or have had inflicted upon them the name, style, and title of 'Modern Athens.'"[2] For the contemporaneous Hungarian traveler Alexander Farkas de Bolon, imagining Philadelphia as Athens was not a casual speculation. He had spent ten days in Philadelphia, the first of them immersing himself in the life of the city, at street level. "The more parts we visited, the more my admiration increased. . . . I thought that I walked in the Athens or the Rome of the classic ages."[3]

Trying out the phrase "Athens of America," it turns out, was commonplace among travelers of the 1830s and 1840s. Travelers may have found that the phrase fit, or that it didn't really fit, as one might have imagined it could have, in the manner of the author of *Things as They Are*. But no one uses the phrase sardonically, as a preface to an irony designed to point out how coarse the Philadelphians really are, how un-Athenian. To imagine Philadelphia as Athens was not flip or facile. And dozens of travelers seriously posed the comparison.

What those travelers are seemingly unaware of is that the phrase had entered the conversation about Philadelphia some years before in the *Anniversary Oration Pronounced before the Society of Artists of the United States* by the great Philadelphia architect and engineer Benjamin H. Latrobe. Speaking in 1811, Latrobe speculates on the relation between the flourishing of the arts and the nature of political power, conceding that often art has been most vigorous when it has been the well-paid recipient of support from an arbitrary, repressive head of state.

Still, it is his conviction that the fine arts are properly at home "in the bosom of the republic." Based upon that belief, he predicts that "the days of Greece may be revived in the woods of America, and Philadelphia become the Athens of the Western World."[4]

The Athenian comparison was one way—there were many—of suggesting a ripe, dense, cultured quality to the city. Specifically, insofar as the allusion is controlled by its various contexts, saying Philadelphia was a kind of Athens was meant to point in several directions. For one thing, some of the dominant buildings of the city were not only Greek Revival; they were aggressively, arrestingly dramatic examples of the style, as if the city had challenged the visitor to compare what he saw with what he imagined to be the art of architecture in the classical past. For another, the city seemed to present, in a way not unlike the high moments of Athenian life, the union of a vital, functional city with a body of humane ideas. For a visitor, remembering Philadelphia as the holy experiment of William Penn and the meeting place of the Founding Fathers, seeing it now as an intelligible, seemingly well governed city, it was quite plausible to see it as special among American cities, the fountainhead of *civitas*, the source of the energies of the Republic, insofar as those energies lent themselves to the art and craft of governing benignly and well.

Beyond this basic assessment, numerous features of the perceived life of Philadelphia contributed to the impression often noted by travelers of an extraordinarily cultivated place, wise in the ways of civilization. Consider the role of Franklin as an emblematic citizen, for example. Taking him to be a figure of virtuosity and insatiable curiosity, stylish and economical in his writing, humble and self-possessed in his person, he comes to embody a synthesis of virtue and erudition. Insofar as travelers seek out his grave, read his epitaph, and remember his presence in the city, as many of them do, he serves to impart an extraordinary dignity to the life of the city, as if its best-known citizen had mastered, above all, the art of living.

Or consider the reputation of the city as home to a multitude of institutions, serving not only as custodians of the marginal but as forces for social experiment. In 1827, Mrs. Basil Hall visits the old prison and the new penitentiary, the "Institute for the Deaf and Dumb," several churches, an orphan asylum, an "Asylum for Poor Widows," the Academy of Fine Arts, the mint, the Navy Yard, the Alms House, the Pennsylvania Hospital, "the Marine Asylum," "the Friends' Retreat for

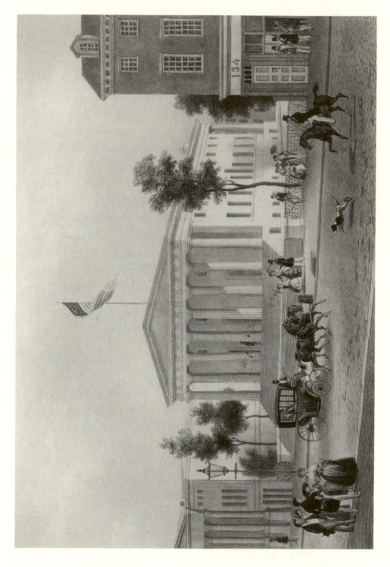

Figure 16. Athenian not only in its cultural tone but in its public architecture, Philadelphia in the nineteenth century is distinguished by its great Greek Revival buildings. Here, in a lithograph by Deroy, the Second Bank of the United States can be seen at the left and in the center, the U.S. Custom House, formerly the Bank of the United States. Courtesy of the Library Company of Philadelphia.

the Insane," an "Infant School," a "Common School." It is not a long
chapter in her book and not many of these places detain her or draw her
into their daily life. Yet there is no mistaking her fascination with the
range and the extent of the institutional life of this rather old, rather
complicated city and the ways that it has devised for taking care of its
own.[5] Few other travelers are as obsessive as Mrs. Hall, or as thorough.
But when, a half-century later, the English traveler Emily Faithfull visits
Philadelphia and takes note of the "School of young Lady Potters," the
women employees at the mint, and the Women's Temperance Union,
one realizes that, while her particular interests are feminist, many of the
same interests as Mrs. Hall's are being ministered to; since Philadelphia
is perceived as a place in which civic virtue is encouraged, decent impulses become converted into institutions, and ways are found for the
city to take appropriate care of those of its citizens who lack the power
to insure their own well-being.[6]

Visitors with a taste for the performing arts often remark on the
range and quality of musical performances in the city – small-scale re-
citals in the first half of the century at the acoustically remarkable
Musical Fund Hall, grand opera in the European tradition after the completion of the Academy of Music in 1857. Travelers often go to the theater: there were two principal playhouses, the Chestnut Street Theater
and the Olympic Theater, and, although the plays and players were often
English, nothing about the experience seems provincial to the travelers.
Visitors interested in the availability of books often remark on the city's
libraries and the accessibility of their holdings to perfectly ordinary
people. No admirer of the literary aptitude of Americans, Captain Basil
Hall does take note of Philadelphia's public libraries – "no fewer than
sixteen" of them in 1824, an extent that seems to him striking.[7] And visitors interested in the production of books often find their way to the
offices of Carey and Lea, or later to Lippincott's, where the city's place
as a center of publishing seems to have been perceived as a quite personal, intimate, intelligible force in the culture of the country.

Beneath all of these perceptions of the high civilization of the city
runs a motif more basic than all of the rest, sometimes implicit and not
elaborated but quite consistent from the beginning of the nineteenth
century nearly to the present time, and that is the idea that the city is an
especially learned place. Some remarkable educational institutions are
thought to flourish in the city together with some singular libraries and
archival collections. A number of conspicuously learned men can be

found, teaching perhaps, writing, bearing witness to the life of the mind. But, more general than all of this, there is imagined to be an apparent erudition in the city at large, a respect for the intellect, which is unlike the life of other American cities.[8]

The French traveler Achille Murat, touring Philadelphia in the 1830s, puts it this way.

The society of Philadelphia is much more enlightened than that of New York; the professors of the university give the tone, which communicates to it, perhaps, a slight degree, almost imperceptible however, of pedantry. The winter parties are meetings of learned and literary people, including citizens in any way distinguished: they are always open to foreigners, properly introduced. Ladies are never present. The meetings are held on appointed days at the houses of different persons in rotation: science, literature, the fine arts, and politics form the subjects of conversation, and in general much intelligence and urbanity are displayed. They are always terminated by a supper, and are calculated to give foreigners a high idea of the intellectual resources of that city.[9]

As Murat makes clear, his conclusions grow out of some particularly happy experiences of his own. Still, he is quite certain that his experiences are not unique: anybody, he thinks, would find Philadelphia distinguished for its intellectual tone. And his conclusions, as I suggest, are not unusual for the mid-nineteenth century.

Murat's observations touch upon several dimensions. One of them is the intimate relationship between the learned institutions of the city and the general tone of its more informed inhabitants. Another is the relationship between the learned life of the city and its social life, with the two being extraordinarily interinvolved. And the third is the accessibility of all of this to the traveler from elsewhere. Of course other travelers read different nuances into the tone of the city. But what seems striking is that Philadelphia, which has always had a reputation for being a somewhat insular, not very gregarious place, its tone being set by its Quaker reserve and its patrician old money, appears here and in others' reports alike as a democracy of the intellect, a rich, egalitarian hotbed of the mind.

Besides that general sense of the intellectual tone of the city and beyond the assessments of the famous learned places of the city, its museums and collections and libraries, travelers, specifically and almost universally, focus upon Girard College. The responses to it are complex and somewhat elusive. But the facts are easily established.

Stephen Girard, an émigré French seaman and small merchant,

had gradually moved into some dramatically proliferating maritime interests, subsequently into banking and urban real estate, ultimately establishing his own bank and even underwriting, at the risk of his entire
fortune, a substantial portion of the War of 1812. After a life of legendary
financial cleverness and some distinguished acts of generosity and sac-
rifice, he died in 1831, having become by far the wealthiest man in
America. His will left a large portion of his estate to the establishment of
an institution for the boarding, care, and education of "poor white male
orphans." Reckoning the exact size of the bequest is meaningless since
much of it was in real estate of undetermined but constantly increasing
value. But clearly it was a bequest in the several millions–millions of
1831 dollars. And it is clear that for a hundred years both natives and
visitors from elsewhere were simply astounded that so much money
should have been given to establish a home and school for orphans. A
survey of the beauties of the city written in 1891, for example, speaks of
the purity of the Corinthian style of the principal building, "a style
which, though both stately and graceful, is hardly appropriate for the
purpose of a school building." [10]

The English officer Arthur Cunynghame, stationed in Canada, traveling in the United States, captures the feelings evoked by the main
building. His enthusiasm is not unusual. Entering the grounds, he
writes that his

astonishment was boundless at beholding a building at once so unique and beautiful as scarcely any country in the world can boast its equal. It was exactly after
the same model as the Madeleine at Paris, but much larger, and *entirely* constructed of the purest white marble, even the roof being composed of the same
material.

The columns are marble; the capitals are marble; the staircases, door-
posts, and landing places are marble. And on either side of the great
center building are two adjacent buildings, also of marble, which are the
sleeping apartments and dining halls of the students, who, he hazards,
"are treated more luxuriously than the sons of the English nobility." The
students' quarters contain warm baths, "drying closets," "hot-air flues,"
"things which at Eton never entered into our philosophy." [11]

Occasionally a traveler will cavil at the building, as being, in some
classic way, imperfect. Captain Marryat calls it "incorrect, according to
the rules of architecture." And the British naval officer Captain Oldmixon thinks that the trustees have made "sad hash of the bequeathed

Figure 17. The city's most intriguing educational institution in the last half of the nineteenth century and the country's most dramatic and expensive Greek Revival building, Girard College appears in Thomas U. Walter's drawing, *Girard College Perspective View* (1835), with Founder's Hall at the center. Courtesy of the Thomas U. Walter Collection, the Athenaeum of Philadelphia.

dollars."[12] But ordinarily travelers are deeply impressed, even over-whelmed. Sometimes an odd enumerative obsession takes over the description, as it does with the waterworks. The Anglo-Scottish traveler William Ferguson, impressed as he might well have been with the fact of a marble roof, is overtaken by the sheer facticity of it all. The roof, he writes, is comprised of 2,046 of the larger marble tiles, each weighing 776 pounds, and 2,061 of the narrow ones, each weighing 214 pounds, giving a total weight of 906 tons. The chimney tops and skylights weigh 20 tons, the gutters $43\frac{1}{2}$ tons.[13]

Surprisingly few observers find much interest in the nature of the education offered at Girard College or the life of the boys there. Ferguson, like Cunynghame, is struck by the facilities: the wardrobes, the presses, the shelves. Sir Edward Watkin observes the clothing, the collective behavior, the discipline, concluding that "the orphan child of the poorest man in the city may come forth with the culture and acquirements of a prince."[14] But visitors to the asylums often draw closer to the inmates and visitors to the prisons often draw closer to the prisoners than visitors to Girard College do to the students. One assumes perhaps that sensitive travelers by the mid-nineteenth century would be drawn to the transformations wrought in the lives of boys struck by misfortune early in life, so that through a benign and enlightened education they could transcend their circumstances. But the students remain out of focus for the visitors and the way they are taught, and what, is of no interest. It is the great building and what it seems to mean and it is the figure of Girard that resonate for the visitor.

Clearly, Stephen Girard leaves many of the travelers slightly off balance. Many of them linger over the clause in his will stipulating that "no ecclesiastic, missionary, or minister of any sect whatsoever" shall ever hold a position at the college or, for that matter, be admitted to its grounds. It seems like a kind of pugnacious secularism, that clause, even though Girard himself explained that the will's intent was rather to shield the students from competing sectarian claims during their formative years. It is, of course, a habit of mind in the nineteenth century to think of philanthropy and religiosity as being inevitably joined. When, as in the case of Girard, an extraordinary act of charity is coupled with the aggressive absence of any explicit personal faith, observers are left with a response that is uneasy and uncomprehending.

But it is the whole figure of Girard that bemuses the travelers, so much so that their language becomes decentered. The encyclopedist

Chambers, for example, is enchanted by many things in Philadelphia; although he is opinionated, he is not ordinarily given to bursts of pique. But the person of Girard and his grand philanthropic gesture move him to a cranky peevishness. The great college building is, he thinks, "a thing devised by the founder to keep his name from sinking into oblivion." [15] Larger than life, Girard is a narcissist to Chambers, cheating death by erecting a Greek temple to himself. To others he is, in some way rarely made explicit but embedded in their choice of language, a figure of myth and legend. When he first arrived in the United States, writes Cunynghame, Girard "was in the character of a forlorn cabin boy, without one dollar in his pocket." A European naïf in the New World, he prospers "by carefulness, good luck, and assiduity." [16] It is not only that Cunynghame's version is preposterous. Girard, in fact, arrived in Philadelphia the twenty-six-year-old master of a French vessel, not a boy, not poor, and not forlorn. It is also that the language of Cunynghame's version is facile and formulaic, like a child's tale from a primer: "without one dollar in his pocket." What Cunynghame knows at some level is that the life of Girard makes no sense to him unless it is cast into a version with familiar features. Making the character of Girard into a little story explains; it supplies a telos; it provides a clarified contour where the outline has been blurred.

More than sixty years after those mid-nineteenth-century travelers, Edward Hungerford gathered his urban impressions under the title *The Personality of American Cities.* His essay on Philadelphia is uncommonly bright and original, fluent and graceful in its style, subtle and sophisticated in its judgments. But in due course, Hungerford turns to Girard College and the person of Girard and he lapses into a language very unlike anything else in his essay—crude, sentimental, moralistic, and tendentious.

The story of Stephen Girard is the story of the man who was not alone the richest man in Philadelphia but the richest man in America as well. But among all his assets he did not have happiness. His beautiful young wife was sent to a madhouse early in her life, and Girard shut himself off from the companionship of men, save the necessity of business dealings with them. He was known as a stern, irascible, hard screw of a man—immensely just but seemingly hardly human. Only once did Philadelphia ever see him as anything else. [17]

Perhaps the ultimate reduction of the complicated figure of Girard to a little story is an anecdote heard and passed on by Richard Cobden, traveling in 1859, in which a less prosperous neighbor of Girard's asks him to reveal the secret of how he has gotten on in the world as well as he has. "'That I will' replied the old millionaire in four words—'mind your own business.'"[18] No one else in the lore of Philadelphia, not even Franklin, invites observers since to recast his life into such coarse and unsophisticated narratives.

Although travelers turn to Girard College in a context that emphasizes its place among the institutions, especially the educational institutions, of the city, it becomes clear that, once faced with the building itself, interest in it as a school, even as a boarding facility, is virtually nonexistent. It is seen as an example of the art of building and of the extension of the will of one inscrutable man. European travelers, of course, are accustomed to sublime and extraordinary buildings as extensions of a single ego and a single will. The sublime experiences that the United States is expected to offer, on the other hand, are natural: Niagara Falls, Mammoth Cave, the Hudson Valley, Yellowstone, the White Mountains. Travelers do not come expecting to find dramatic buildings. When they find that great Parthenon on the fringe of the city, their astonishment is palpable. Discovering Girard College is not without its reservations. Dickens remarks that if the unfinished marble structure is completed according to its original plan, it will be "perhaps the richest edifice of modern times." But the terms of the legacy are in litigation, he adds, the work is stopped, and so "like many other great undertakings in America, even this is rather going to be done one of these days, than doing now."[19] But even Dickens's rather dour disposition during his Philadelphia tour and his pessimistic view of American projects cannot obliterate the fact that he too is caught up in the general amazement at the grandeur of the building: "perhaps the richest edifice of modern times."

It is not surprising, perhaps, that an interest by travelers in the intellectual tone of Philadelphia, its quality of mind and its institutions, is transformed, as the city becomes revealed, into an interest in buildings. There is, however, a feature of the intellectual life of the nineteenth-century city that has nothing to do either with buildings or with mythic figures with storybook lives. Thomas Hamilton's account of his visit in 1843 is sharply observed but not very generous, supercilious in the manner of more than a few British travelers in midcentury. But early in his report of Philadelphia life, he mentions, first, his attendance at a meeting of the American Philosophical Society, then his participation in something called "Wistar Parties." The first has pleased and impressed him. Established by Franklin as an informal meeting in a tavern and continued ever since, it continues to be convivial while including in its meetings many of the finest minds of the country. His response to the Wistar Parties is more complicated, partly because he has never seen anything like them.

Held by rotation at the houses of the members, the Wistar Parties, named after the member at whose house they were first held, include persons of accomplishment in various fields, literary and scientific, who gather, eat, and converse. The quality of mind in such meetings Hamilton finds impressive; and the general temper he finds charming. There is as much eating as there is talking, a situation that lends itself to a respect for difference and a tempering of acrimony. "No man can say a harsh thing with his mouth full of turkey, and disputants forget their differences in unity or enjoyment." [20]

Remarkably, the meetings seem to be open to members of all classes. The merest "operative mechanic" who shows an interest in learning and conversation is welcome. And while there is more than a little condescension in the description of what happens to such a person – "his errors are corrected, his ardour is stimulated, his taste improved" – the democratization of a kind of salon experience is remarkable to Hamilton. So, for that matter, is the fact that he, Hamilton, is there. It seems to have been the case that visitors to the city with any claim to distinction in science or letters would become known as being visitors and subsequently would be invited to the Wistar Parties without an elaborate introduction.

A few years before Hamilton's visit, Basil Hall had lived through the same experience, with comparable pleasures. He arrived in Philadelphia on November 30, and by the next day he had been invited to a Wistar Party. There, he is surprised and delighted by the combination of a generous and graceful social occasion with a stunning gathering of intellect and erudition, surprised and delighted, as well, to find himself so hospitably received. A week later, he returns. This time he meets the eminent philologist Du Ponceau, whose work he knows. Du Ponceau, it turns out, also knows Hall's work on the East Asian languages and he gently and respectfully corrects a basic error in Hall's argument. [21] Much of what Hall comments on in his travels has a ritual, obligatory effect to it: there is the thing to be seen; he sees it; and he fashions a response that seeks to be judicious, stylish, attractively sensible. His response to the Wistar Parties is different. It is clearly an experience that he could not have anticipated. And he is engaged and moved by it in a very personal way.

In the long run, the number of travelers who actually participated in the Wistar Parties could only have been infinitesimally small. The number of Philadelphians who could be invited to a given party was only twenty. And although the number of strangers was not limited, these were, after all, dinner parties at a private home and there could hardly have been over twenty more. But those who did visit were famous and often literary, often influential in their opinions. And if the fame of most of them is faded now—the naturalist von Humboldt, for example, and the duke of Saxe-Weimar—some are not—Thackeray, John Quincy Adams. Whatever their enduring fame, many of the visitors wrote about the experience, and what they wrote was read. And so for a century, the Wistar Parties came to be seen as a defining aspect of the culture of Philadelphia.[22]

By the early years of the twentieth century, that sense of Philadelphia as a special place in which erudition and intellect were honored and cultivated had begun to fade. It is not so much that those qualities of mind and culture were no longer visible and valuable. It is rather that other places in the United States had become at least as eminent. Philadelphia could no longer seem so unusual as it became increasingly obvious that a growing number of university communities, some in quite unlikely places, provided research facilities and opportunities for the exchange of learning far beyond anything dreamed of in the gentle world of the Wistar Parties.

It is easy to find contexts in which those old judgments concerning the mind and culture of Philadelphia would have been advanced but are not, the writer remaining silent on the intellectual tone of the city. The Anglo-Irish man of letters Shane Leslie, for example, came to the city in 1934 to occupy an endowed chair at the University of Pennsylvania. He lectured widely, visited the historical city, saw much art, and met several famous people. Surely along the way he would have met any number of figures from the university, would have visited, perhaps, the American Philosophical Society or the Library Company, would have formed some opinions concerning the vitality of publishing in the city at the time, would have measured the sophistication of the audiences for his lectures. But one waits in vain for that assessment of the tone of the city that would have been so customary a century before. Whether addressing the intellectual vitality of the city is a level of generalization that would have been temperamentally congenial to Leslie or not, it is something to be said about the city that has simply gone out of fashion by 1934.[23]

A half-century later, the *National Geographic* published a pictorial essay on the city called "They'd Rather Be in Philadelphia." The photographs are enchanting and so is the text, as it moves between broad views of various aspects of the city and a sharply focused engagement with a single person: there are the cultural institutions and there is an interview with Eugene Ormandy; there is local taste in food and there are the words of Jeanne and Daniel Sidorick, bakers of soft pretzels; there is the Italian Market and there is Joe Giordano, former boxer and fruit vendor. Almost no sense of problem enters the description of the city—no violent crime, no poverty and homelessness, no drugs. In an essay that seeks to put the best face on Philadelphia, presenting it as vital and complex, above all interesting, the writer would surely have stepped back and offered up a generalization on the intellectual tone of the city, if such a thing seemed appropriate to say any longer. But it is clearly a way of seeing the city that has long since served its time and nothing remotely resembling those old descriptions of Philadelphia as a haven of erudition appears.[24]

All travel writing is one half of a dialogue. What we read are the answers. The questions that provoke those answers are buried, only implied. Behind those nineteenth-century descriptions of the "Athens of America," lies the question: Is the United States a cultivated place, in which scientific inquiry is encouraged, literary grace is valued, and the powers of mind given an honored place in the life of the culture? It is a preposterous question to imagine asking now or at any time in the present century. But it was not a preposterous question in the century before. The answer was, of course, that, by and large, the United States was nothing of the kind, being a vast, complex country still quite crude—except for the surprising and happy discovery of Boston perhaps, of New York perhaps, but above all of Philadelphia.

8

Loathing Philadelphia

Speaking ill of Philadelphia is so rich and extensive a tradition, so old and continuous, so clever and ingenious at times, so dull and predictable at others that merely gathering all of that bad mouth together would fill a book. Two centuries ago, as the yellow fever epidemic decimated the city, it was commonplace, and justifiable, to imagine Philadelphia a terrible place to be. Through its various falls from grace in the decades since, there have always been reasons to find the city torpid or backward, ludicrous or irrelevant. But the ease with which the city has been mocked and defamed transcends the reasons for it: there is a will to believe ill of the city that always outruns the facts. W. C. Fields probably never spoke the line "On the whole, I'd rather be in Philadelphia"; in any case, it is not inscribed on his tomb. The sentence first appeared in *Vanity Fair* in the 1920s and seems not to have been ascribed to Fields until after his death.[1] That the attribution is probably erroneous seems oddly uninteresting. What *is* interesting is the power and persistence of the line. Making a dry, condescending joke about Philadelphia has seemed so right to the millions of people who have heard the line, believed it to be factual, and repeated it through the decades that the vigor of the sentence and its triumphant credibility are more important than its dubious attribution.

Disparaging Philadelphia is different for those who do not live in the city and those who do. Sidney Fisher, a mid-nineteenth-century aesthete, diarist, and lifelong resident, loved Philadelphia: it sustained his need for a layered, structured city and a wide circle of cultivated, affluent friends. That much is implicit in every page of his diaries; he rarely actually says so. On those occasions when he writes explicitly about the city, however, his tone becomes bitter and hyperbolic and his style, normally a fluid middle style, takes on the rolling parallelism of a jeremiad. The city, he writes in 1842, is as stupid as a village in the West.

"No society, no life or movement, no topics or interest of any kind. . . .
The streets seem deserted, the largest houses are shut up and to rent,
there is no business, there is no money, no confidence & little hope."[2]
Twenty-five years did not temper his affinity for writing in that mode. In
Philadelphia, he writes in 1867, "there is no literature or appreciation of
it or literary men or appreciation of them. The whole tone of public
opinion is opposed to intellectual culture of any kind, which is dis-
couraged & any manifestation of it rebuked by the narrow jealousy of
ignorance."[3]

What is striking is not that Fisher loves the city or that he hates it
but that he does both more or less simultaneously with such uncompro-
mising vigor. For a long time before Fisher and ever since, residents of
Philadelphia have tended to feel as he does. However complicated and
ambivalent ordinary life in the city may be, when it comes time to for-
mulate opinions about it, to capture in a few judgmental words a sense
of Philadelphia, a stark, antithetical contrast emerges: love and hate. The
great amateur historian of the city Ellis Paxson Oberholtzer, for example, formulates his version of that bipolarity in the introduction to his
Literary History of Philadelphia. The city, he writes in 1906, is afflicted
with unclean streets and wretched paving, "vile water and politics," a
totally unpredictable climate. Yet it is unaccountably beloved by its citizens. "No community in America has the same compelling power over
its inhabitants."[4] In the 1970s, the city adopted a promotion campaign
that briefly encapsulated that classic duality in a single, public slogan:
embarrassed and apologetic, at the same time proud and loyal. "Philadelphia," the slogan read, "isn't as bad as Philadelphians say it is."

Visitors and travelers, of course, people contemplating the city from
a distance or for the first time, have no reason to feel that bipolar response. They may love the city or hate it and sometimes they seem to do
both at once. But the loving lacks the irrational tenacity of the native and
the hating lacks the Philadelphian's weary masochism. For visitors, the
loving and hating are often expressed quickly, without much density or
complication. Matthew Arnold loved the city. It takes him two sentences
to tell how. "Philadelphia," he writes in 1884, "is the most attractive city
I have yet seen over here. I prefer it to Boston."[5] On the contrary, Kate
Chopin, in 1870, found the city instantly loathsome: all the people looked
like Quakers, the streets looked like Quakers, and "the very houses re-
semble them with their odious brick fronts, and those everlasting white
shutters!"[6]

Figure 18. A brief and unsuccessful campaign in the 1970s to purge the city of its derogation. Courtesy of Urban Archives, Temple University, Philadelphia.

Chopin's derogation of Philadelphia is stylish and evocative in its description so that it is difficult not to be captivated by it, even if one thinks it terribly unfair. It seems original and observed, done with a novelist's eye. But surely something more complex is the case than merely clever observation. Although she was then only in her early twenties, she was uncommonly sophisticated, with her own ideas about variety and uniformity, decoration and austerity in the life of cities. Although her reaction to the prospect of a Quaker city is, no doubt, quite genuine, it is all but certain that she had formed an idea of what a Quaker city was going to look like before she arrived, knew, moreover, how she was going to like being in one. Writers before and since Chopin have used Quakerism to flog the city. It seems not at all unreasonable to say that of all of the ways of reacting to a city, speaking ill of it is the most imitative and traditionalized. Writers, reacting negatively, build, usually without conscious intent, upon what they have heard and what they have read.

Nobody knows how old that rich tradition of speaking ill of Philadelphia really is. But it is well established by the beginning of the nineteenth century. The Irish poet Tom Moore provides a curious base point. Moore was apparently a figure of considerable charm, famous and stylish, eager to please, easy to like. Although he spent only about ten days in Philadelphia during 1804, he wrote fondly of the city in his correspondence and set several of the poems written during that time within Philadelphia locations. A legend grew and persisted that he had lived for a time in a cottage on the banks of the Schuylkill, although no evidence has ever supported the tradition. Two years after his visit, however, he published some notes accompanying a volume of poems, in which he comments on having found the common run of Americans to be ignorant, uncultivated, and corrupt. And his Philadelphia audience, having lionized him, took his latter opinions personally. In the midst of these bruised feelings, an anonymous author, purporting to be Moore, wrote a piece for the *Literary Magazine*, broadly burlesquing the supercilious opinions of American places characteristic of European visitors. It was far from obvious at the time that the piece was burlesque. Indeed it is not obvious now. The piece is clearly hyperbolic, but such remarks are always hyperbolic, whether intended as a joke or in all seriousness. And American readers, Philadelphia readers particularly, bruised once by Moore, imagined themselves to be bruised a second time.

The essay opens by pronouncing Philadelphia "the most dull, monotonous, uninteresting city on the face of the globe." And then the author finds his rhythm.

It wants more churches, market houses and coffee houses. Its churches, few as they are, want steeples and their steeples want bells. They also want audiences and their audiences want zeal. Their choirs want singers and their singers want voices. Their markets want space, air and shelter, and their coffee houses want room, dignity and convenience. The streets want variety, being too uniformly wide and straight. Of the only curved streets, one is too narrow and the other is too wide.

The houses are all wrong, too high, too low, the hotels too dirty and dark, the theaters barnlike, devoted to cheap entertainment, the public buildings vulgar and pretentious. If the satiric intent of the piece seems so stylized and overdone as to be totally obvious, consider this sentence.

There is no reverence for the past, no institutional continuity, complains the author, and "the hall of the Revolutionary Congress is now a depository for stuffed birds and beasts." The criticism seems harsh, intemperate, and meanspirited. But one reflects on the fact that it was quite true. The second floor of Independence Hall was indeed given over to the museum of Charles Willson Peale and the city did display an appalling indifference to the preservation of its historic places. A reader then who missed the idea that the piece was a hoax and who imagined its intent to have been quite serious would have had ample reason to have done so.[7]

Moore was in due course exonerated of the authorship of the piece. But his shifting fortunes in the affection of Philadelphians is of no interest now. What is interesting is what the furor establishes. For the burlesque to have been taken seriously in 1806, it was necessary for it to have been totally plausible, more-or-less familiar, the kind of thing that visiting Europeans could be counted on to say, shocking only because it seemed to have come from the beloved Tom Moore. Clearly, the possibility of derogating Philadelphia on grounds of its stupifying monotony is a tradition at least two centuries old.

In that list of complaints by the anonymous impostor, nothing is amusing, except perhaps for the numbing parallelism of the invective. Churches without steeples and markets without space are not funny. The strand of the catalog of failures that suggests mediocrity, monotony, and torpor, however, is potentially amusing. Had the anonymous author wished to generate laughter at the expense of Philadelphia, he could have refashioned his observations on dull churches, dull streets, dull buildings, dull citizens into anecdotes and tall tales. That was not his intent in 1806. But in the century that followed, it was that strain of preposterous jocularity that became predominant, jocularity based upon the perception of a bland monotony. It is not only that travelers really seem to see that quality in the life of Philadelphia, but also that such a level of observation lends itself to a particular kind of wit–apparently clever and penetrating, also supercilious. A traveler who came to Philadelphia and made a joke about being there, situated himself above the city, in a position of amused, cosmopolitan condescension. And that is clearly where more than a few visitors to the city wished to locate themselves.

When Captain Marryat remarked that, arriving in Philadelphia, he imagined that it was Sunday when in fact it was not, he has given, after all, a wonderfully economical expression to a perfectly hilarious idea:

the idea that the second city of North America, an extraordinary center of culture and commerce, should seem to be so vacant that its inhabitants would appear either to be in bed or in church. There is an oral, "told" quality to Marryat's line, as there always is with jokes about the torpor of Philadelphia. The timing counts not perhaps for everything but still for very much. The substance of the joke is hyperbolic and extravagant while the tone of its telling is dry and understated. The tension between the two is absolutely essential to the effect.

Almost a century after Marryat, Philip Gibbs, an English traveler, reports a Philadelphia joke, told by New Yorkers. When he arrives in Philadelphia, he finds that the joke was quite misleading: the city is very far from the torpid place he had been led to expect. Still, he is plainly amused by the joke; he does repeat it. Philadelphia, say New Yorkers, is "so slow that it was safe for people to fall out of windows—they just wafted down like gossamer."[8]

That tendency, to discount the pertinence of the Philadelphia joke while savoring the telling of it, is not unusual. A few years before Gibbs's experience of the city, Charles Henry White, writing a sweetly affectionate profile of the city for *Harper's*, frames his essay with a Philadelphia joke. It is not that he thinks the joke appropriate; actually he thinks it rather stupid and misapplied. But such a reputation so surrounds the city that he feels obliged to acknowledge it. As a man's train is leaving for Philadelphia, a stranger on the platform runs along beside the car, "butting into people, getting his hat punctured for his pains," until, even with the passenger's open window, he calls out, writhing with mirth, "Good-by . . . have a good sleep!"[9] Again, one notes that, although the figure in the story is an oaf and although White thinks the anecdote terribly unfair, he does relate it with color and energy.

It is really quite amazing, that commerce in bad jokes. William Archer, the dominant theater critic of the English-speaking world at the turn of century, a man of great wit and erudition, a tastemaker, traveling from New York to Philadelphia, sets down the requisite Philadelphia jokes. They seem neither clever nor amusing now and one searches Archer's text in vain attempting to discover how Archer found them either funny or apposite. To a famous New York wit, says Archer, "is attributed the saying, 'Mr. So-and-so has three daughters—two alive and one in Philadelphia.' Six different people have related this gibe to me." A little later, Archer recounts the well-known anecdote of the Philadelphian visiting the doctor, complaining of insomnia. The doctor advises him concerning diet and exercise, adding "'If after that you haven't better nights, let me see you again.' 'But you mistake, doctor,' the patient replied; 'I sleep all right at night—it's in the daytime I can't sleep.'" [10]

It was the golden age of the Philadelphia joke, the first decades of the twentieth century. By then all of the possible variations had been played out on a very narrow set of themes. And the form had reached a distilled perfection. Writers defensive of Philadelphia during the period often tell such jokes with a sigh of resignation, so as to get them out of the way. "We have heard more times than we can count," writes Elizabeth Robins Pennell, the wife of the great illustrator, "of the Bostonian who retires to Philadelphia for a complete intellectual rest, and the New Yorker who when he has a day off comes to spend a week in Philadelphia and the Philadelphian who goes to New York to eat the snails he cannot catch in his own back yard." [11]

As recently as 1980, Edwin Wolf, surveying the long history of the derogation of Philadelphia, ends by citing the familiar sentence "I spent a week in Philly one Sunday." Those weary and empty bits of jocularity at the expense of Philadelphia seem to hang on, Wolf complains, beyond all reason.[12] Even as Wolf was writing his essay, however, the whole phenomenon of joking at Philadelphia's expense had undergone some remarkable changes. For one thing, the city, during the midcentury decades, had undergone various waves of reform and regeneration. However much of this revitalization was apparent to people based elsewhere, it had begun to become clear that automatic condescension and scorn were no longer appropriate responses to the city. Those old jokes about sleeping in Philadelphia become very hard to find in print after the forties. They were not only rarely written down, but one assumes that they gradually ceased being told. Those jokes represented a vein of humor long since painfully imitative and played out. They spoke to a Philadelphia that had, for some time, been in the process of becoming unfunny.

What gradually comes to replace the Philadelphia joke as the principal form of derogation can be found in two representative observations at the turn of the century. Beatrice Webb, an English traveler of progressive politics and extraordinary intellect, recorded her impressions of the city in a diary of 1898. Her critique of the political life of the city is trenchant and clear-eyed. But what is rather more durable than her description of the workings of municipal government is her novelist's eye for the people involved. Observing the chambers of the city council, for example, she is far from oblivious to the issue before that particular session and the play of power involved in its success or failure. But what really captivates her are the bodies, the voices, the faces in that small drama of municipal politics American-style.

> We attended a session of each chamber; the members were a low looking lot–All the same, these ward politicians have a certain distinction of physiognomy–they are forceful men: a strange combination of organising capacity, good fellowship, loose living, shrewdness and strong will. . . . The appearance of these town councils is in a sense more distinguished than one would expect to see in an English town council noted for corrupt dealings; at once more distinguished and more degraded. The well-shaped head and prominent eyes, heavy jaws, self-confident and easy manner, ready tongue, make many of the ward politicians far more attractive and interesting species of parasites than the seedy little nondescript shame-faced persons who, in English Local Government happen to be open to corrupt influences.[15]

Her host, a local journalist, is disappointed that she is not more impressed with the accomplishments of local government, the extent of the water system, for example. "We replied that every other person seemed to be recovering from typhoid fever! (The water is taken direct from the river)." Discussing the rather mindless awarding of a patronage job on the basis of party loyalty, the local politician to whom she directs her question answers "with something as near a wink as the heavy stupidity of his countenance permitted."

Part of her obviously admires the unapologetic venality of it all, the coarseness, the ease in the use of power. In balance, she does not seem to find the city ill-governed. But what obviously strikes her as most memorable about the way in which Philadelphia is governed is the bloated, ham-fisted gallery of rogues who are actually doing the governing.

Beatrice Webb's notations were diary entries; they were not published during her lifetime and had no audience. Observations such as hers were nonexistent in an earlier period. The fact that she wrote them at all indicates a shift in the way in which a traveler from abroad might see the city. But five years after her descriptions of the politics of the city, the muckraking journalist Lincoln Steffens toured the city and wrote about it. And his description, not terribly different in its sensibility from Beatrice Webb's, did achieve instant fame and durability, as memorable as anything ever said about the city.

Appearing first in *McClure's* in 1903, subsequently collected as a pivotal segment of his *Shame of the Cities*, Steffens's essay carries a title that, in a sense, says it all: "Philadelphia: Corrupt and Contented." Steffens knows the tradition of the Philadelphia joke, that dry, supercilious anecdote, told at the expense of stupid Philadelphia. Nothing, of course, could be further from his own purpose than the continuation of that tradition. One Philadelphia joke, however, does seem to him worth repeating because of the appalling implications that it quite clearly carries and the equally appalling fact that it is told not by people from elsewhere, to the derogation of Philadelphia, but by Philadelphians, about life in the city. And it seems, both to those who tell it and those who respond, not troubling, actually rather funny. It is said that, once, "a party of boodlers counted out the 'divy' of their graft in unison with the ancient chime of Independence Hall." [14] Unamused, Steffens notes that the hallowed traditions of national origin still preserved in the city–the great hall, the chambers, the famous bell–coexist alongside a political venality that is total and without exception. The amused complacency, moreover, that accepts, within the same frame, Independence Hall and "a party of boodlers" counting the profit of their graft seems to Steffens supremely emblematic of the degradation of the democratic process in the governing of the city.

Reading Steffens at this distance, nearly a century later, the persons whom he finds so contemptible–Matthew Quay, Dave Martin, "Stars and Stripes Sam" Ashbridge–the multiple and blatant occasions of fraud, the issues and the conflicts, all of these are faded beyond recovery. The essay is extraordinarily alive, all the same, and what makes it so is rather like what energizes the notations of Beatrice Webb. The essay is extremely novelistic. It is partly his cast of characters. They are such brazen crooks; there is a kind of Beggars' Opera aspect to their shameless self-dramatization. It is partly Steffens's feel for particularity–the concrete detail, the rhythms of the spoken language.

J. C. Reynolds, the proprietor of the St. James Hotel, reports Steffens, went to the polls "at eleven o'clock last elections day, only to be told that he had been voted." Steffens is quite understated in his use of the jargon of graft. To *be* voted. It means, of course, that some party hack has appropriated the name of a legitimate voter and cast a vote for the machine candidate. When the citizen appears, a vote, his own vote, is no longer available to him. He has been voted. Mr. Reynolds asked

how many others from his house had been voted. An election officer took up a list, checked off twelve names, two down twice, and handed it to him. When Mr.

Reynolds got home he learned that one of these had voted, the others had been voted.

So it goes, as Steffens's cast of lowlifes and machine functionaries systematically deprive the electorate of its franchise. A jocular sense of the sleepy city persists into the twentieth century. But that is not the principal form of derogation. Rather the dominant form becomes Steffens's, or some variant of it—Philadelphia as a place in which the sleepy complacency has consequences that are dark and sinister.[15]

Not surprisingly, Mencken's *American Mercury* in the twenties and thirties contains the most memorable examples of the mode. With the title of a 1939 essay "Philadelphia: City of Brotherly Loot," one knows where one stands. The city, begins the author Alan Frazier, is broke, its debt overwhelming, its equipment in deep disrepair, its urban climate pervaded by racketeering and prostitution. The centerpiece of the essay is a guided tour of the extravagant, ill-conceived, and wasteful projects undertaken by the municipal administration: an abandoned tunnel under the Schuylkill River, a marble administration building of the board of education, "on which $3,000,000 was spent at a time when 2000 school children were in part-time classes because there were not enough schools."

In 1918 the City Fathers built a tube under Locust Street for three blocks, spent $1,000,000, and then forgot the whole thing. In 1931 a new set of City Fathers decided to build a subway, also in Locust Street. When they dug they discovered the old one. It was "too small" so millions had to be spent tearing it out. Now Locust Street subway No. 2 also has been abandoned. It is there today, a $5,000,000 hole in the ground, without trains and without tracks, leading from nowhere to nowhere.[16]

Frazier's essay is not without its moments of amusement, the result of a flair for invective that Frazier has obviously learned from Mencken. It is also not without its moments of hope and it ends by describing the sources of reform and regeneration that may prevail against formidable odds. But its tone, thirty-five years after Steffens, is still Steffens's tone.

If traces of that mode can still be found, the witty invective, the corruption uncovered, it has long ceased being the dominant mode of maligning Philadelphia. Something else has gradually replaced it in the last thirty years, with a tone more dark than anything before. Consider a group of exhibits.

First, a book by Michael Middleton called *Man Made the Town*, published in Great Britain and subsequently in the United States, on the problems and possibilities of continuity and change in cities. Not really a coffee-table book, its text is substantial and provocative, meant to be read, it is, nonetheless, beautifully illustrated, largely in color, with photographs of urban scenes, many European, some American, all designed to illustrate the possibilities of the human use of cities, their regeneration and reconstruction, along lines that invite the eye and speak to the possibilities of a street-level engagement of inhabitants and environment. Nearly all of the photographs beckon, seeming to invite the casual reader of the book, who might well say, implicitly, page after page, There is a place in which I could enjoy walking, sitting, working, being, living for a time. The imaginative use of city centers most engages Middleton, the plazas, squares, and arcades that provide the light and color and space that make life in cities a sensuous pleasure.

There are, of course, some counterexamples, a garish storefront, a clutter of neon, an aerial view of parking lots. But none of these illustrations of urban ugliness so affront the eye as the first of these counterexamples. It exists in a double-page layout illustrating the unity of buildings and setting. There is an ancient French walled town, a Greek mountain village, Norwich cathedral, Chicago's North Shore. The sun shines in these pictures and the colors vibrate. The natural and the made coexist in perfect equipoise. Off to the side of the double page stands the single counterexample. The bottom half of the picture is street, half in shadow. It seems to be late afternoon on a hot day. The volume of litter on the street is immense. And the trash has been there so long that it has lost all character: looking like many lumps of papier-mâché, the trash has no identity, having become aging, generic litter. The top half of the picture shows a crudely made brick wall, straight enough but pointed without care, containing several enormous windows fitted with iron bars. Through the windows appears nothing at all, or rather more trash, no interior; only what seems to be a freestanding wall separates the filthy street in front from the filthy street in back. No people exist in the picture and it is impossible to imagine what a person might be seen to be doing there. But in the center of the picture stands a shabby and sagging velvet sofa, meant to be elegant in its time, its stuffing oozing out of a corner, its legs broken. It is somehow shocking and disturbing, that abandoned sofa amid such urban desolation. Middleton's text, at that point, reminds the reader of what any view of urban regeneration filters out: the public housing and abandoned cars, the mo-

notony and decay. And the sofa photograph is obviously intended to remind us that in any city, if we attend to niceties of design, other, ugly
things are simultaneously going on. But it is the caption of the picture
that is doubly shocking to someone from the eastern United States.
"Philadelphia, Pennsylvania," it reads, identifying the location of what
serves in Middleton's book as the primary, emblematic example of urban obscenity.[17]

Second, an exhibit from a different mode: Two years before Middleton's book, in 1985, the movie *Witness* appeared. Tightly directed by
Peter Weir and quite powerfully acted by a strong cast, it combines a
drama of crime, detection, and police procedure with a study of the clash
of two cultures, the Pennsylvania German culture of Lancaster County,
popularly the "Pennsylvania Dutch," and the gritty, urban culture of
contemporary East Coast cities. The opening scenes develop the first of
these polarities: gently blowing grain fields, seen at the eye-level of a
person standing among them, small groups of the local inhabitants,
dressed in their characteristic clothing, the white farms, a funeral, the
grieving, resilient women. Soon the idyllic imagery becomes mixed
with the strident artifacts of contemporary life – the rural view contains
a roadside Dairy Queen, the horse and buggy share the road with a
sixteen-wheel tractor-trailer. And the rural world begins to fade away as
an Amish mother and her young son board an Amtrak train, arriving
shortly afterward in the city.

The camera moves between the boy's eyes, wide and without guile,
to the details of the train station, which the camera sees at the level of
the child, a world of exaggerated height, oddly filtered light, and
strangers, all of whom are seen to be at least unusual, at most sinister.
To the casual viewer of the film, with no knowledge of the cities of the
eastern United States, it would perhaps be unclear where the action
is now taking place. But the mother speaks of her destination, which is
Baltimore, suggesting that the city where they are now shown to be,
which is between their rural home and their destination, is surely Philadelphia. Residents of the city recognize the specific scene at once as
Philadelphia's 30th Street Station. In any case, the location is made clear
a few minutes later when the character played by Harrison Ford names
the city.

The event that drives the plot occurs as the boy, in the toilet stall at
the men's room, witnesses a particularly grisly murder through a
slightly open door. The Amish world of the opening scenes is still in the

viewer's mind. And so the murder demonstrates how great a distance it is, forty miles perhaps but a vast moral gulf, from the gentle farms of Lancaster County to the sordid and dangerous public spaces of Philadelphia. The murder, it turns out, is not a random crime or an isolated instance but an episode in a fabric of corruption that includes a substantial portion of the Philadelphia police force. Nothing links Michael Middleton's book on urban development with Peter Weir's film about Amish innocence and contemporary degradation, except that each of them, at a crucial point, chooses, for an exemplary image of urban hell, the city of Philadelphia.

A third exhibit. The recent work of the documentary photographer Eugene Richards, ultimately a book, received its greatest currency as a small portfolio of some dozen photographs in the quarterly *Granta*. They are harrowing. In a grainy black and white, with the informal centering of a spontaneous, hand-held technique, they show the intervention of policemen, mostly white, into the lives of the black inhabitants of an inner-city neighborhood. The events portrayed are largely arrests and interrogations. Sometimes the badges, the holsters, the handcuffs, the leather of the police are so prominent in their centrality to the picture that they seem light sources. There is no light in the crumbling background of boarded up doorways, graffiti, and littered streets. The faces of the police are at once tentative and assertive, sometimes clearly afraid. The faces of the residents are suspicious, mocking, defeated. Nothing redeems the desolation of Richards's series.

The accompanying text describes the "War Zone" that the photographs portray. It is so called "from the fact that most of the people who live in it are armed." Almost all of them, grandmothers to children, are also involved at some level in the business of crack and heroin. The text briefly describes the visits of the photographer. "During his first visit, he witnessed three people dying on the streets; their deaths were unnatural ones and were the result not of police brutality or of gang shootings but of the killing strength of the drugs available." Despite highly publicized wars against drugs, there is no evidence of any such campaign in the War Zone. Policing, the text concludes dryly, "is inadequate and underfinanced, and most officers enter the War Zone with the greatest reluctance."[18]

The subject matter of Richards's series and its tonalities clearly show an older eastern city: the brick row houses make that clear. The photographs could have been taken in Baltimore or Newark. But they were not. And Richards wishes to make it clear that they were not. The title of the series is "Philadelphia."

The idea that speaking ill of Philadelphia should have taken such an ugly turn seems, at first, more than a little puzzling. It is not that it seems ill-founded as a response to the experience of the city. Moving outward from City Hall in any direction, one encounters vast areas of appalling decay and obvious threat. Urban decay, however, is a general condition of our time. Most American cities in the last forty years have decayed faster than they have regenerated. Yet Philadelphia is capable of being singled out, imagined to be evil and ugly in a special way. Another exhibit suggests a plausible reason for such a dark distinction.

In 1993, Jonathan Yardley published his personal travel book through the mid-Atlantic states, which he called *States of Mind.* As he makes clear at the outset, Yardley's own connection to the city is extensive. Two centuries of his ancestors have lived in or near the city. And Yardley himself visited often when he was a teenager and his grandmother lived in Chestnut Hill. Revisiting the city now, he brings an immense baggage of family connection and personal reminiscence. And much of what he sees now is heavy with recollection of childhood. A warm, genial, accepting tone plays over much of what he observes about the city, and even when he is displeased by what he sees, he is rarely angry or troubled.

All of that changes, however, as he travels Germantown Avenue toward Chestnut Hill, carrying the memory of the street in the fifties—its trolleys, its cobblestones, its prosperous shops.

Never in my experience has a clash between memory and present reality been more dramatic or disheartening. The trolley cars were still there, and the cobblestones, but from Hunting Park Avenue to Chestnut Hill all else was a war zone. Beirut. Dresden. Saigon. Storefronts were battered, boarded up; those that were open presented a wary eye to the world, while those that were closed hid behind protective layers of wire. The day was bright yet almost all the colors seemed bleak, defeated, faded; weeds overran empty lots, graffiti soiled walls and doors.

For three or four miles this grim procession continued; at its end I was heartsick, in this instance not so much because of my own sense of loss but because of what we as a community have abandoned and destroyed in our rush to the bland lawns of suburbia.[19]

Yardley's melancholy conclusion suggests the principle that underlies that tendency to discover a special degradation in the decay of considerable areas of Philadelphia. Even when they do not consciously know it, observers of the city carry with them a sense of what the city once was, both as a mythic place embedded in the texture of American experience and as a happier place in living memory. Placing the question in a moral frame, the observer from elsewhere, seeing the city, can feel it to be especially depraved. Placing the question in a material frame, the observer may well feel the city to be especially decayed, deprived, down on its luck. Philadelphia is no more deserving of such a dim view than any city of the Northeast with a largely departed industrial base. It is simply that Philadelphia is where Franklin lived and where Jefferson invented the Republic, and where visitors from abroad found, for a century, a gracious and sophisticated city. If it seems now especially fallen, it is because it has had longer to fall, and farther.

9

Dreaming Philadelphia

For many years in the forties and fifties, the *New Yorker* ran an advertisement, its format resembling a full-page *New Yorker* cartoon. It was always drawn by Richard Decker. Its medium was always the same: a public scene rendered in ink and wash. And the caption never varied. "In Philadelphia," it said in bold italics at the bottom, "nearly everybody reads The Bulletin." So like a *New Yorker* cartoon these drawings appeared to be that the magazine saw fit to clarify the intent by printing "Advertisement" in parentheses below the caption.

Two examples from 1950 can demonstrate the basic premise. The illustration of March 18 portrays the waiting room of a maternity ward, so named on the door. Some dozen expectant fathers, sleepy, unshaved, and smoking, are, instead of waiting for the baby, reading, with total absorption, the *Philadelphia Bulletin*. The obstetrician can be seen through an open door, reading the *Philadelphia Bulletin*. And the nurse, carrying the newborn infant, is reading the *Philadelphia Bulletin*. Only a slender, nervous man in a black suit, bald, with a long, pointed nose, is *not* reading the *Bulletin*, is, rather, paying apprehensive attention to the baby, whose cries engage him but fail to penetrate the attention of everybody else, so exclusively absorbed are they with their newspapers.

In the February 4 illustration, the view is of a theater, from the rear, looking up the center aisle toward the stage, on which an actor and an actress are in postures suggesting the possibility of high romantic emotion, except that both of them are reading the *Philadelphia Bulletin*. In the seats of the theater are the patrons; one sees the backs of their heads. But instead of watching the action on the stage, each one is holding the *Philadelphia Bulletin*. Only a single figure, the familiar man in the black suit, with the long nose and the bald head, leans into the aisle from his seat, attempting to see the action on the stage, not an easy thing to do since his view is blocked by everybody else's newspaper.

The advertisements were conceived and generated by N. W. Ayer, then of Philadelphia, later of New York, surely among the two or three most ingenious and enterprising ad agencies of the century. The agency must have been persuaded of the success of the series; it did, after all, run for a very long time. And the clients at the *Bulletin* must have been pleased, imagining that the advertisements drew both attention and revenue to the newspaper. Yet from our distance now, it is impossible to comprehend the intent. The advertisements are mildly amusing now, seeing how many variations can be wrung out of a single joke. But what is most likely to strike a reader of those advertisements at our distance from them is the uncompromisingly derogatory view that they carry of life in Philadelphia. Faced with the unexpected, or the dramatic, or the exciting, or indeed the life-threatening, Philadelphians, the ads seem to say, cannot be roused from their daily papers. It is the evening *Bulletin* that provides all the engagement with life that Philadelphians can stand. Experience itself is simply not interesting. More hostile than any of those shaggy jokes about trying to stay awake in Philadelphia, the advertisements' portrayal of the whole sensorium of Philadelphia life is devastating.

Yet there is something oddly compelling about those ads. One's ability, now, to respond to such a quality depends upon a willingness to take them as occupying a plane that their creators surely never intended them to occupy. They are, in some quite convincing sense, dream scenes, night scenarios. They are as convincing as they are because they enact a pattern that is universal, or seemingly so. Dreams in which the central dramatic element is a gulf between a crisis occasion and the human response to it are, as everyone knows, commonplace. Although someone is falling, or running from an assailant, or drowning, although the train is out of control, the elevator cables have broken, or the gorilla has escaped, no one is paying any attention. No one understands such simple words as Look! or Help! or Watch out! It is not that there are no other people. There are many other people. But none of them is able to enter into the urgency of the situation. It does not matter whether one engages those pictures from the point of view of the nervous man in the black suit, all the other inhabitants of the city sleepwalking through life with a newspaper in front of their faces, or whether one sees them from a distance, as an unfolding drama in which one has only a spectator's interest. In either case, one is drawn into a dream scene and the locus of the dream is not the calm and sheltered suburbs of Philadelphia, not even the neighborhoods of Philadelphia; rather the dream is enacted in

In Philadelphia nearly everybody reads The Bulletin

Figure 19. One of a long series of cartoon advertisements in the *New Yorker* in the fifties and sixties. Only the nervous man in black is attentive to the unfolding drama, everyone else anesthetized by the *Bulletin*.

the very center of the city itself, where the population is densest and the energy level is highest.

Compare those bizarre dream scenes of the mid-twentieth-century *New Yorker* with the experience of a British traveler of the Civil War period, Edward Dicey. Already disoriented by the ferocity of an American winter, further threatened by the movement of the Army of the Potomac and the uneasy feeling that he might be engulfed by hostilities at any time, Dicey travels south from New York to Philadelphia. He takes the mail train, which arrives at two o'clock on a winter morning. Nervous about his luggage, he has kept his baggage check, determined to keep track of his bags. Yet, sleepy and confused at so odd an hour in the morning and knowing nothing of the city, he has decided simply to wait for whatever omnibus would appear that might take him to an agreeable hotel. He waits in vain. There is no omnibus, no private carriage, no transportation at all, except a streetcar that would take him to the train to Washington. Since that dubious streetcar is the only transportation available, he determines to take it, gathers his baggage with great difficulty, and boards the streetcar, asking the conductor, as he climbs aboard, to recommend a hotel. The conductor is civil but totally unhelpful, as he drops Dicey off at a corner, advising him that, within four blocks, he would probably find a hotel.

I don't know that I ever felt a more helpless individual than on that winter morning at two o'clock, in the streets of Philadelphia. I had a most indistinct notion of which way I was to go. Whether four blocks meant four, or four hundred, or four thousand yards, I was unable to guess. There was not a soul on the streets, and I had a huge portmanteau, two large carpet bags, a bundle of heavy wraps, and an umbrella, to transport with me.

He sits on his luggage, hoping someone will appear to help. Of course, no one does. On his own, he carries first his trunk for a small distance, then comes for his bags, then again comes back for his wraps and umbrella, repeating the procedure several times, all the while concerned that he might meet either a thief or an uncomprehending policeman.

However, in the main street of Philadelphia at two A.M., I met neither thief nor policeman, nor living soul; and after an hour's labour I reached an hotel, considerably the wiser in the art of American travel by the night's experience.[1]

The events as Dicey relates them are plausible and no one would imagine he had invented them. Even now, Philadelphia is inadequate in its signs and it is, like most American cities, not easy for a stranger to negotiate at 2:00 A.M. Yet Dicey imparts a chilling inner quality to the experience so that hearing him tell it is to hear the strangeness of it all, a haunting dislocation that *feels* like something far more bizarre than merely being in an unfamiliar city at an odd hour. Like those *New Yorker* ads but with a different set of tonalities, Dicey's narrative reads as if it were the recollection of a dream. Like the figure in the black suit, he is agitated and alone. Like the Philadelphia of the *New Yorker* ads, the city is unaware of his presence. The arrival in Philadelphia, as he describes it, might have been an opening scene in a movie by Buñuel or Bergman in mid career. And Kafka, Gogol before him, and a hundred writers in their wakes, might have written it. We use the word "surreal" too easily and casually in our own time. Still, something about Dicey's experience, and his account of it, has converted the plain city of Quaker habits and straight streets into a dream scenario.

So much of what Philadelphia has always presented to the visitor is rational and orderly: the image of Franklin and the Founding Fathers, the Quaker reserve, the row houses and the straight streets. There is, of course, a different dimension or a counterreality. One counterversion, the one of the last chapter, is the idea of Philadelphia as a ridiculous place, dull and inept, evil and corrupt. But there is a different counterversion. And it is the imagination of the city as a dream.

Seeing Philadelphia as if it were a dream comes about in two different ways. First, the ordinary mind, confronted with certain sensory dimensions of the city, its light, for example, which visitors sometimes describe as being hazy or blue, experiences a momentary view that seems not really of the waking world, even though one knows well enough that it is. The outlines, in lights at night, of the boat houses on the Schuylkill, seen from across the river is a happy scene dulled by familiarity for most residents of the city but startling, magical, and dreamlike to the visitor. An announcement of an arriving train, incomprehensible in the reverberations of 30th Street Station, sounds like a voice out of the private drama of one's night world, even though one knows perfectly well what is happening at the time. In the mid-nineteenth century, visitors to Belmont Mansion in Fairmount Park discovered that the location of the great house provided a view to the east that included not only an attractive prospect, a gentle decline toward the river valley, but also a portion of the skyline of the city, distant yet immediate somehow, the tops of the buildings appearing to emerge from the trees in the middle distance. Ever since, engravers and photographers have sought to catch not just the visual contours of the view from Belmont Plateau but something of its hallucinatory effect, the city seeming to hover over the trees, near enough to invite but far enough, like a mirage, to be unreachable.

The other way of dreaming the city is to fasten on some experiential aspect of its life, allowing that aspect to generate an obsessive drama of the urgencies and anxieties of life in Philadelphia. That is what the *New Yorker* advertisements do. And the unfortunate Edward Dicey recalls his bad night in Philadelphia as a parable of urban callousness and indifference, narrated with a nocturnal set of tonalities.

In a sense, it was Penn himself who first dreamed the city, before the fact. From the start, he advertised his city as being spacious and healthful, verdant, safe from fire, a contrast to the sorry cities of Europe. It was visionary to have done so. The city did not exist at the time that he spoke of it in such terms. Residences were to be no closer than a quarter of a mile from the rivers, assuring a permanent fringe of parkland. Large, broad main avenues would be laid out, as well as four squares, preserved as permanent parks. And lesser streets would be plotted, parallel and straight, numbered.

No one has ever maintained that Penn's imagination of the city literally came to him in a dream. But even after Penn and his conception of the city have faded into the past, his imagination of Philadelphia has had about it a strongly visionary tone, as the various legendary versions of his inventing of the city tend to emphasize. One legend, for example, has maintained that the name of the city derived from an Egyptian pharaoh, Ptolemy Philadelphus. Another proposed that Penn had decreed that a space within the city should remain forever vacant so that Indians would always have a place to camp. And another held that the grid plan determining the layout of the city's streets had been borrowed from ancient Babylon.[2]

Still, the really gripping visions of the city are those that dream it as a collective social pathology: the catatonic Philadelphia of the *New Yorker* and Edward Dicey. The mere mention of a collective social pathology suggests the stereotypical imagery of genre fiction, the urban bad dream that underlies crime fiction since Dashiell Hammett and Raymond Chandler. If Philadelphia seems a less likely setting than other more obviously sinister cities, it is, all the same, quite sinister enough. "We drove into the city, past rows of boarded-up stores, Laundromats,

Figure 20. The skyline viewed from Belmont Plateau, appearing as if a dream, seemingly suspended in the clouds, just above the trees. Courtesy of the Library Company of Philadelphia.

bars, and discount shoe shops." So reads a recent piece of such genre fiction, a bad-dream crime novel that might have been set in any aging American city, except that it happens to be set, specifically, in Philadelphia. "Mackenzie did a smooth slalom around the iron supports of the elevated lines on Market Street."[5] For a reader who knows Philadelphia, the iron supports of the Market Street elevated rail line give a small stab of recognition to the moment. For a reader from elsewhere, the scene partakes of the twilight world of a hundred similar fictions of the last seventy-five years.

But when such dream fictions of social pathology are not the typical features of a subgenre, derivative and self-imitative, but are, instead, eccentric and original, they can be quite affecting. The narrator of Ford Madox Ford's *The Good Soldier*, John Dowell, for example, projects an extraordinary example of the city as a major center of population and culture in which paranoia is not an aberration but the norm. He has been in Florence, he tells us, long enough to have forgotten such banalities as fashion and greed or the nature of a dollar and the desirability of having some dollars if you happen not to, forgotten also that "there was such a thing as gossip that mattered." In that respect, Philadelphia, he recollects, was "the most amazing place I have ever been in my life." He had been in the city for only a week or ten days when he realized that he had been warned innumerable times by everybody against everybody else. "A man I didn't know would come up behind my lounge chair in the hotel, and, whispering cautiously beside my ear, would warn me gainst some other man that I equally didn't know but who would be standing by the bar."

The purpose of this conspiratorial whispering is never clear. Possibly, he muses, these figures imagined him to be in pursuit of some large financial deal, concerning the city's debt perhaps or the ownership of a railroad. His reasons for being in Philadelphia are, in fact, unremarkable. He owns a few properties, which he wishes to see. And he has a few relatives in the city, whom he is pleased to renew his acquaintance with. They are pleasant people of modest means. "They would have been nicer still if they hadn't, all of them, had what appeared to me to be the mania that what they called influences were working against them." In any case, he carries away the impression of a city containing aging houses with old-fashioned rooms, more English than American in their style, the rooms being dominated by "handsome but careworn ladies," who talked "principally about mysterious movements that were going on against them."[4] Like all dream visions of the city, Ford's narrator's passing reflections grow out of a commonplace observation about Philadelphia, that it has always been a rather closed and gossipy place, less cosmopolitan, more insular than other cities of a similar size. Like other dream visions, Dowell's stylizes and extends those recognized features, in his case into an amazing world of shared and interlocking paranoia.

Those dreams of Philadelphia do not really prepare a reader for the movement through the city of the narrator of Peter Handke's remarkable "Short Letter, Long Farewell." The experience of Philadelphia occupies a small portion of the narrative, but it is so strange and haunting that readers of Handke are not likely to forget it.

The narrator grounds himself in the dislocations of postwar Europe and the particular unease of a broken marriage and a deeply troubled private life. Moving through the American landscape, always with a view toward finding Judith, his wife, he brings to the journey not only an extensive knowledge of the surface details of American culture but a complicated and incisive sense of the uniqueness of the American character, grounded in his reading of the novels of F. Scott Fitzgerald, for example, and the films of John Ford. The train ride from New York to Philadelphia establishes the mode, at once recognizable and hallucinatory. As unpredictable interludes of light and darkness play over the vision of the area surrounding the railroad, the images begin to assemble themselves: "garbage heaps instead of houses, yellow smoke but no chimneys, a car without tires lying upside down in a fallow field. . . ." Arriving at the city underground, he takes the escalators up to ground level.

On the street, his prevailing mood is nervous apprehension. As he watches, two Quakers dressed in long black coats and broad, flat hats cross the square and prepare to enter a car. A marine, whom the narrator remembers from the train ride, moves toward the Quakers and shows them something. They smile, one of them makes a negative gesture, and they get into the car. "Then he got out again and pointed at me. I was frightened. They motioned to me and I went slowly toward them. The marine raised his arm and brandished my camera; I had left it in the train."[5] It is an odd pastiche, with elements that are contemporaneous and other elements that are anachronistic: the Quakers, for example, are figures from an imagined past, not from the street life of postwar Philadelphia, or perhaps more likely, they are figures from the picture on the carton of Quaker Oats, conflated with the knowledge that Philadelphia is sometimes known as "the Quaker City."

Intensely conscious of the way in which his gestures are likely to be read by others, the narrator makes every attempt to read the gestures of those around him. They seem to act out a code, the key to which he does not possess. Language is not an issue since not much is said. But the merest physical movement is problematic and self-conscious. "Can people see that among many gestures I always have to choose one?"

He idly watches the television in his hotel room: a man in a chef's hat, an animated cartoon in which a cat blows bubblegum. At length he emerges again at street level. And by now even the most orderly features of Philadelphia seem menacing and deeply disturbing. "In Philadelphia the streets run parallel or at right angles to each other. I went straight ahead, turned into Chestnut Street, which is one of the main thorough-fares, and then again went straight ahead. The streets were all very quiet." Fragments of inexplicable violence intrude upon him. And that vague texture of inscrutable gestures surrounds him. Soon he moves on, westward, to the small town of Phoenixville, leaving an image of the city more troubling than those dream visions of an earlier time, as troubling as it is because it is not really possible to tell how much of the sense of Philadelphia Handke's narrator has plausibly rendered from the data of the city and how much he has projected from his own unstable sense of self. But what is most disturbing–startling and unanalyzable–is the picture of the Quakers walking in nineteenth-century Quaker dress in the concretely rendered Philadelphia of the 1960s, like elements in a composition by Magritte perhaps, or as if some cosmic practitioner of collage had cut and pasted illustrations from an old book into the liv-ing rhythms of a modern city. In some uncanny way, Handke's version of the city evokes an estranged, anomic quality that is as plausible an interaction of the visitor in Philadelphia as all of those happier, self-possessed interactions of the centuries before.

Many of those classic features imputed for two centuries to Phila-delphia by those who do not live there can, it turns out, serve as the premises for an invention that casts the city into the twilight zone. Per-haps any city could be so imagined. Certainly Philadelphia, for all of its reputed matter-of-factness, can, at moments, seem mysterious, and even in broad daylight it can seem dreamed. But there is one aspect of Phila-delphia that is altogether different from any other city.

Consider the traditional, familiar names for American cities. The Windy City, the Motor City, the Mile High City. These are names devoid of resonance, factoid names, as if devised by some idle positivist. There is Chicago. It is often windy there. It is the Windy City. Motors are made in Detroit. Let it be called the Motor City. Contrast those empty nicknames with the single urban epithet that partakes of the visionary, so familiar now that we do not really hear it any more, the City of Brotherly Love.

T. Coraghessan Boyle's novel *East Is East* propels a Japanese sailor who has jumped ship off the coast of Georgia into a collision not only with American culture as a whole but with a daunting range of subcultures—affluent retirees gathered in their shore-home enclaves, indigenous rednecks, a writer's colony, the law-enforcement establishment, local and federal.[6] Half-American by birth, Hiro, the sailor, holds out a slim hope that he might find his father, an army veteran of whom he knows almost nothing. A half-breed in Japan and thus a pariah, he hopes to feel less ostracized in the ethnic stew of the United States. What he very much wishes to find are the artifacts of American life that he has come to know from the movies and television: armchairs, end tables, and thick carpets; crime and degeneracy and a crazy freedom; cowboys, hookers, Indians; cheeseburgers; ranch houses. But what he most wants to find is home. And the phrase that offers him that possibility is "The City of Brotherly Love."

It is not that he has been to Philadelphia or that he expects ever to be there or that anything he has been led to believe induces him to expect that in Philadelphia all men are brothers and that, as a consequence, they love each other. It is not that he has any concrete notion of what the city contains. It is rather that the name of the city is a visionary concept, suggesting a haven, a dreamscape.

American culture yields Hiro no accommodations. And the episodes of the novel, though comic, are dark and painful. When he dies, demoralized and defeated, Hiro carries into death the unfulfilled vision of Brotherly Love. Far though it may be from the troubled world of coastal Georgia, there is a place where brotherly love exists. Hiro knows that, even though he does not know how to get there. And so Boyle's eccentric and compelling novel comes to rest on the one dream of Philadelphia that does not change because it is not dependent upon the actualities of the city at all. Rather it is dependent upon an ancient moral vision invested in an old city, embodied in a nickname that no one really hears any more, yet a nickname, all the same, that names a dream of human, urban possibility that is plainly astonishing.

L'envoi: Thirty-six Views
of Philadelphia

Rosy Light and Perfect Enchantment

The river makes a bend just above the water-works, and the curving banks scooping themselves form a lovely little sunny bay. It was more like a lake, just here, than a flowing stream. . . . The golden sky, the mingled green, brown, yellow, crimson, and dark maroon, that clothed the thickets; the masses of grey granite, with the vivid, mossy green that clung round them; the sunny purple waters; the warm, red colour of the road itself, as it wound down below, with a border of fresh-looking turf on either side of it, the radiant atmosphere of rosy light that hung over all; all combined to present a picture of perfect enchantment. The eye was drunk with beauty.

–Fanny Kemble, *Journal*, 1835

Summer Heat

Whether deservedly or not, Philadelphia enjoys the reputation of being the hottest city in the Union, the feature in question greatly contributing, during summer, to the comfort of its inhabitants, the streets lying in one direction, being constantly in shade, which, with the exception of a short period, at noon, may also be said of those intersecting them. The value of this may be appreciated, when it is understood that, in summer the thermometer sometimes rises to above 100 Farenheit in the shade. It rose to 104 one Sunday that I afterward spent there, when, if a breath of air swept by, it gave little relief, feeling more like a hot blast than otherwise.

– Alexander Mackay,

"A British Traveler in Philadelphia," 1849

Invariably Rainy Saturdays

If I were to write a history of Philadelphia, according to the profound spirit of investigation for which modern tourists are remarkable, I should say that it was a peculiarity belonging to its climate, that Saturday is invariably a wet day.

—Fanny Kemble, *Journal*, 1835

Frogs

The streets of Philadelphia all run parallel, or cross each other at right angles, and many of them are planted with a row of trees on each side. In walking along them, I was a good deal entertained with the loud, and almost incessant chirping which is heard from the trees in the evening, after sunset; and which I understood was chiefly occasioned by the tree frog. This species of frog makes its abode amongst the branches of the trees, and makes a very considerable noise in the evening.

–Robert Sutcliff,

Travels in Some Parts of North America, 1804

Squirrels

I have already spoken of the Squares or GARDEN ENCLOSURES of Philadelphia; and really I know no more pleasant treat, after a long walk through
the hot and dusty streets, than to rest oneself in the shade of one of these
prettily planted gardens, cooled by the plashing of water from numerous
gardens, and gaze on the deer quietly grazing, perfectly tame and uncon-
scious of the bustle around. While I was seated thus, one day, I felt a
curious sensation, as if something larger than a spider or mosquito was
stealthily climbing up my back, and on heartily arising, I found that I
had disturbed a fine squirrel, who, however, came in front of me, nothing daunted, as soon as I resumed my seat, and begged for biscuits and
nuts, usually given to these pretty creatures by good-natured loungers.
He next leaped into my lap, and extended his paws, as if for my donation;
but, unfortunately, I had gone out unprovided with the accustomed gifts.
I patted and stroked him, therefore, but this would not serve his purpose; so, giving me a look of disdain and pity, he leaped down and
speedily ensconced himself in the lap of some one near, whom, perhaps,
he would find more generous than myself. All these squirrels are very
tame, for they seem to enjoy an immunity from the pranks of mischie-
vous boys, such as we have in England; and they are regularly fed by the
city authorities, as well as by the bounty of private individuals.

–Alfred Pairpoint,

Uncle Sam and His Country, 1857

Quakeresses and Weeping Willows

I should say that Philadelphia would be improved in appearance if more of the religious edifices had spires attached to them; and there is a general air of somberness about it, increased perhaps by the quantities of Quakeresses and weeping willows you meet at every turn.

–Lieutenant Colonel A. M. Maxwell,

A Run through the United States, 1841

A Clean and Bountiful Market

Probably the market of Philadelphia displays the greatest quantity of fruits and vegetables in the world. Boat loads are brought by the Delaware, and numerous wagons come loaded from the interior. Peaches, apples, pears, melons, cucumbers, pine apples, sweet potatoes, onions, &c are plentiful beyond example.

The cleanliness and the civil address of persons who vend provisions in the market are truly gratifying: if a speck is to be seen on the white apron of the butcher, it may be inferred that it came there on the same morning. Girls arrive on horseback, or driving light waggons, to sell vegetables, or the produce of the dairy. Many of these females, I am told, are the daughters of farmers who are in good circumstances. Here are none of the lazzaroni hucksters of fruit and sweet-meats, that form such a deplorable spectacle in the finest cities of Britain.

–James Flint,

Flint's Letters from America, 1820

Immaculate Butchers

No one, who has not seen it, can form an idea either of the variety, abundance, or neatness, of the Philadelphia market. . . . Nothing can exceed the whiteness of the benches and stalls; the meat, which consists of every sort, is exquisitely neat, cut with the greatest care, smooth, and disposed upon tables, on cloths as white as the whitest cambric. The butchers wear a white linen frock, which might vie with a lady's wedding dress. . . . The butcher stands at his table, the woman sits in her stall; no moving except that of the citizens, who are coming and going continually from early in the morning till nine o'clock at night. The whole of this mighty scene is conducted with perfect order; no contention, no strife or noise—presenting one of the most interesting sights perhaps in the world.

–Mrs. Anne Royall,

Sketches of History: Life and Manners
in the United States, 1826

Large Women

The ladies in Philadelphia are, generally speaking, much taller than most American women, and I think the men have the same preeminence in size, but it is more remarkable in the women.

–Mrs. Basil Hall,

The Aristocratic Journey, 1827

Beautiful Women

I have already said that the women of New York are very ordinary; those of Boston I found considerably more attractive; but the ladies of Philadelphia are charming, and indeed superior in point of beauty to most in Britain, coming nearer to those of Italy than any that I have seen, although their features are very different.

–James Logan,

Notes of a Journey through Canada,

the United States of America and

the West Indies, 1838

Noise

We came to Baltimore, *via* Philadelphia; and though I very much admired the regularity of the Iron City's streets, and the beauty of many of the principal buildings, its profusion of white marble, and its perfection of cleanliness, I was glad to escape from its unearthly nightly noises. . . . All night a sound, as of a masque and procession of one hundred menageries let loose, filled one's ears . . . while bells, horns, gongs, and rattling fire-engines, helped to swell the hideous chorus.

–Lady Emaline Stuart Wortley,

Travels in the United States Etc., 1849

Fire Alarms at Night

Before I leave Philadelphia, let me add that I have lost a great deal of
sleep in it, by the almost nightly alarms from fire, this arises from the
old houses being built of timber, and such is the terrible uproar made
by the fire-men and boys, dragging their patent hose or fire engine along
the pavement, and their unceasing yell of fire, that no sleep can resist it
but the sleep of death.

-E. Howitt,

Selections from Letters Written during
a Tour through the United States, 1819

Gangs, Graffiti, and False Alarms

The districts, especially of Southwark and Moyamensing, swarm with . . . loafers, who, brave only in gangs, herd together in squads or clubs, ornamented with such outlandish titles as "Killers," "Bouncers," "Rats," "Stingers," "Nighthawks," "Buffers," "Skinners," "Gumballs," "Smashers," "Whelps," "Flayers," and other appropriate and verminous designations, which may be seen in any of the suburbs written in chalk or charcoal on every dead-wall, fence and stable-door. . . . One of their favorite tricks is to raise a false alarm of fire and then make a rush for the engine-houses, pushing aside the regular firemen and assuming their places at the ropes. In this way they gradually usurped control of two or three engines and apparatuses, and finally drove away the respectable members of the companies, who chose rather to give up their property than to incur the disgrace of such ruffianly association. . . . Previous to the Mexican war and the shipping of large numbers of these rowdies as volunteers . . . , every few nights these companies would contrive to come out, upon a false alarm, and go through with their devilish orgies, throwing brick-bats, spanners and paving stones about in all directions and yelling through their detestable "fire-horns" as if Satan and all his journeymen had come up to do a little spreeing altogether too disgusting to be permitted in their native regions. Frequently these scenes were prolonged all night, driving sleep from every pillow in the neighborhood and filling the hearts of old grannies and women of both sexes with terror and despair.

−George G. Foster,

"Philadelphia in Slices," 1848

Permanency

I returned home to dinner, on the whole pleased with the appearance of Philadelphia. There is something solid and comfortable about it, something which shows *permanency*. Every thing looks neat, the steps are white, the entries clean, the carriages nice, the houses bright. All this betokens perhaps too nice attention to the minutiae of life, but the effect upon the eyes of strangers cannot be denied to be cheerful and inviting. I think I should like to live in Philadelphia.

–Charles Francis Adams, *Diary*, 1834

Dirty Streets

Needless to say, the city is poorly lighted, horribly dirty, and badly kept, particularly in regard to the cleaning of the streets. All seems to be calculated so as to disgust the citizens from getting around except in omnibuses. The streets, barely reinforced by a system of ballasting—neither macadam nor paving—offer a series of hills and valleys likely to injure pedestrians and break the carriage springs. Not a street is free from tracks. All are surrounded with one or several railroads. These railroads, which we call "American" railroads in Paris, do nothing else but confiscate part of the public way for the profit of a particular organization, calling it "for general use."

—Lieutenant Colonel Camille Pisani,

Prince Napoleon in America, 1861,

Letters from His Aide-de-Camp

Clean Carpets

The streets are covered with sheets of pure ice, rendering it dangerous to walk on them. I asked why sand or ashes were not strewed on them, and was told that visiters would bring it into the houses on their feet and dirty the carpets! They may break their limbs by falling, but the carpets must be preserved unsullied.

–George Combe,

Notes on the United States of North America
during a Phrenological Visit, 1838

Overheated Rooms

How, for example, am I able to communicate a just notion of the intelligence, the refinement, the enterprise of the Philadelphians – their agreeable and hospitable society, their pleasant evening-parties, their love of literature, their happy blending of the industrial habits of the north with the social usages of the south? All this must be left to conjecture, as well as the Oriental luxury of their dwellings, and the delicate beauty of their ladies. I only indulge in the hope that these fair and fascinating beings will not accuse me of want of gallantry in hinting to them, in the gentlest possible manner, that they have one fault – at least I think they have – one, however, common to all their country-women, and that is, staying too much in the house, in an atmosphere not quite, but nearly, as hot as that of an oven. O these terribly suffocating apartments, with the streams of warm air rushing out of grating from some unimaginable hot cavern beneath – siroccos of the desert led, as a matter of fancy, into drawing-rooms – languor-promoting and cheek-blanching gales – enemies to health and longevity! How the ordinary duties of life are carried on in these hot-houses, I cannot understand.

–William Chambers,

Things as They Are in America, 1854

Musical Instruments in the Philadelphia Climate

An Italian gentleman mentioned to us, that the climate of Philadelphia destroys musical instruments imported from Germany or England. He had an excellent pianoforte sent to him from Germany; but the first summer dried up the wood so thoroughly, that the keys would not act, and the instrument became useless. He hoped that the winter would restore it; but was disappointed. The German instruments are not varnished, but polished. The air takes off the polish, and in one year the naked grain of the wood appears.

−George Combe,

Notes on the United States of North America

during a Phrenological Visit, 1839

The Metropolis of Prejudice

In the course of conversation, the Governor spoke of the prejudice
against colour prevailing here as much stronger than in the slave States.
I may add, from my own observation, and much concurring testimony,
that Philadelphia appears to be the metropolis of this odious prejudice,
and that there is probably no city in the known world, where dislike,
amounting to hatred of the coloured population, prevails more than in
the city of brotherly love.

–Joseph Sturge,

A Visit to the United States in 1841

Proper Ladies

Many of the innovations which are to be met with daily in cities like New York and Baltimore are not tolerated here. For instance, "society ladies" do not attempt to paint their faces and improve their natural charms, after the fashion set by many of their sisters in other places. A leading doctor in Philadelphia told me that a Baltimore lady who was staying here lately attempted to walk down Chestnut Street as she did at home, but found herself subjected to comments which were far from pleasant, and was obliged to abandon the rouge which she could indulge in freely elsewhere, as she was fortunately unwilling to place herself in a mistaken position. . . . A healthy spirit of activity and desire for mental culture prevails, and the Philadelphia ladies are first and foremost in all good works.

–Emily Faithfull,

Three Visits to America, 1884

Quakers at the Dance

All Philadelphia was astir to see Fanny Elssler, who danced this evening. She is in the same hotel with me. I was much pleased with her dancing, but what amused me as much was to see the hall crowded, and to hear the furious applause, far exceeding London or Paris, and that at Philadelphia, the chief city of the Quakers–Quakers wildly excited over the dancer Fanny Elssler. The theater is neither large nor well arranged; on the first row were many very pretty women, all young, and dressed so exactly alike, that one would have taken them for sisters had there not been so many of them.

–Chevalier de Bacourt,

Souvenirs of a Diplomat, 1885

Sunday in Philadelphia

Immediately after breakfast I went to the Exposition, not remembering that it was Sunday. Now on Sunday the Exposition is closed, the stores and the restaurants as well, everything closed in this happy town. How gay it was! The few people you met were coming from church with funereal faces and their Bibles in their hands. If you were unfortunate enough to smile, they stared at you with flaming eyes; if you were unfortunate enough to laugh, they would have had you arrested.

–Jacques Offenbach,

Orpheus in America: Offenbach's Diary of
His Journey to the New World, 1876

No Echo from New York

Philadelphia is a city very peculiar–isolated by custom antique, but having a good solid morality, and much peace. It has its own dry drab newspapers, which are not like any other newspapers in the world, and contain nothing not immediately concerning Philadelphia. Consequently no echo from New York enters here–nor any from anywhere else: there are no New York papers sold to speak of. The Quaker City does not want them–thinks them in bad taste, accepts only the magazines and weeklies. But it's the best old city in the whole world all the same.

–Lafcadio Hearn,

Elizabeth Bisland, *The Life and Letters of Lafcadio Hearn*, 1889

Nothing Inflammatory

When Mr. [George W.] Child bought the "Ledger" of Philadelphia he ex-
cluded from its columns all reports which could not be read in a family,
or that poison and inflame the passions of young men, and all scandal,
slang, and immoral advertisements. He doubled the price of the paper,
and increased the rates of advertising. The paper was at a low ebb when
he took it; it sank lower now. His friends warned him that this would
never do; that popularity meant sensation; that common people would
not buy common sense, nor would advertisers prefer a journal of good
taste. Nevertheless, Mr. Child went on. He engaged good writers, paid
good wages, and made a great paying paper. People in England would
not expect this could be done in America. I know nothing in journalism
more honorable than Mr. Child's sagacity and courage herein, or to the
good sense of the people of Philadelphia who gave their support to this
unwonted and unexpected exercise.

-George Jacob Holyoake,

Among the Americans, 1881

More Happiness Per Head

After the others, Philadelphia strikes you as beyond all things a civilized city – a city where people sometimes have a little leisure. Elsewhere they do business or seek pleasure; here they live. The very names of the streets – Chestnut, Walnut, Vine, Spruce, Pine – have a fresh and wholesome breath about them. It may be fancy, but the women here seem prettier and the men better set up. The New Yorker takes a tram-car to go a quarter of a mile, and grows fat; here the physical type is more athletic. The richer Philadelphians live out in the country and ride to hounds; the poorest rides a bicycle. The typical American woman's face – long, thin, pale, pure-eyed, like an early Italian Madonna – is here richer and less austere. Middle-class you may call the place, with its endless rows of sober red brick; but middle-class with little of dowdiness, and much of rational stability. If there are few notable buildings, there are few slums. If few people are very prosperous, few are very wretched. In sum, the Philadelphians get more happiness out of their city than any other townsmen in America.

–G. W. Steevens,

The Land of the Dollar, 1897

Touching the Past

There is enough of interest in the friends one makes in a day's idling among the floating population of this quaint corner to leave a lasting impression of the Philadelphian's happy capacity for an intelligent appreciation of an infinite number of things apart from the mechanical daily routine. It is this civic character of the Philadelphian that forms such a startling contrast between him and his matter-of-fact brother in New York. His mode of living, the happy tradition of his environment, and the fortuitous conditions which enable him to touch the past at innumerable points are largely responsible for it, and make it a common occurrence for the Philadelphian to daily pass the house formerly occupied by his grandfather as a matter of course, while we New Yorkers, who have long since sold our grandsires' bricks to the wrecking firm, pass them without a twinge of conscience.

–Charles Henry White,

"Philadelphia," 1906

The Living Penn

It is at least as possible for a Philadelphian to feel the presence of Penn and Franklin as for an Englishman to see the ghosts of Alfred and Becket. Tradition does not mean a dead town; it does not mean that the living are dead but that the dead are alive. It means that it still matters what Penn did two hundred years ago; I never could feel in New York that it mattered what anyone did an hour ago.

–G. K. Chesterton,

What I Saw in America, 1922

Vaudeville Laughs

Philadelphia is certainly the largest city in the world whose very name, mentioned all by itself on any vaudeville stage, brings forth a spontaneous laugh.

— Alphonse B. Miller, "Philadelphia," 1926

The Fitness of Things

There is an abiding sense of the fitness of things—an almost British sense of conformity—about the town, which is not wholly accounted for by the Quaker preciseness of its founder. Penn was after all a conspicuous protestant against the formalities of the English church and court and he brought with him to the promised land a most un-English company of Swedes, Germans, French, Irish, and Welsh. Perhaps there is something in the atmosphere—that makes for the doing of the right thing in the rightest sort of way.

—Frederick Lewis,

"Philadelphia," 1927

Bleak November

Philadelphia, a metropolis sometimes known as the City of Brotherly Love but more accurately as the City of Bleak November Afternoons.

−S. J. Perelman, *Westward Ha!* 1948

The Absence of Color

Was it New York, looming just over the horizon which sent a chill shadow over this city?

One is forced, for explanation, to invent private theories. Do Philadelphians suffer from a kind of native malady which induces dullness and a certain apathy, a mass vitamin deficiency perhaps, one of the sort whose need in spiritual nutrition has not yet been established? Because, though time has indeed darkened this city, there is a dinginess to it that years alone cannot account for. (Think of the brightness and color of far, far older European cities.) Your trolley will travel on and on through drab, red brick sameness, through noisome slums that have spread like a creeping fungus. The trolley has no name; all too often it goes to much the same sort of place it has come from. To live here is like imperceptibly sinking in quicksand; it requires all one's energies to remain stationary.

–Hollis Alpert,

"Philadelphia: Plans and Pigeons,"

Partisan Review, 1950

Municipal Water

Finally, water. Philadelphia drinks its own sewage. The City of Brotherly Love is, in fact, the only one of similar rank in the nation where the quality of the drinking water is a compelling problem. Both the Delaware and the Schuylkill are indescribably filthy rivers, slimy with industrial and human waste. One expert recently termed the Port of Philadelphia "the largest, vilest, and foulest fresh water port in the world"; its water is so tainted that, literally, it damages the steel walls of ships. Every day, some 500 million *gallons* of raw sewage pour into the rivers that are the city's only source of water. To create a proper supply, and to avoid the necessity of chlorination which affects the taste of the local water even though making it safe enough, would cost 150 million dollars. The industrial plants upriver would have to change their techniques in getting rid of waste, which is at present simply dumped into the rivers, and so several of their owners oppose projects for amelioration and reform.

–John Gunther, *Inside U.S.A.*, 1951

Food for Days and White People Serving

While we were visiting, they held a Horn and Hardart picnic out at Woodside Park. Aunt Rose's husband, Uncle Henry, bought some tickets, and the whole tribe of us took the trolley and went to the park. That picnic really floored me; I'd never seen anything like it. There was food for days, and everything was free. . . . That day at the picnic, I ate so much ice cream, and to top it off, white people were serving us and smiling and I had never seen that before.

–Dizzy Gillespie,

To Be, or Not . . . to Bop, 1979

Neighborhoods in 1900 (and 1950)

In 1900 there were few people in the five boroughs of New York who had never been to Times Square, few people of the working-class suburbs of Boston who had not seen the Common, few people in vast Chicagoland who had not visited the Loop. There were, in 1900 (and even in 1950), many Philadelphians who had never walked in Rittenhouse Square, in spite of the considerable network of trolley lines across Philadelphia (where public transportation was corrupt but sufficiently ample). Many, perhaps most, of the inhabitants were quite uninterested in the people, the buildings, the institutions of another neighborhood, sometimes only a mile or so away. When an Irish Catholic boy from Manayunk married a Polish Catholic girl from Port Richmond, his people spoke of a Mixed Marriage. If his brother, also from Manayunk, a parishioner of St. John the Baptist, married a Polish Catholic girl from St. Josaphat's, two hundred yards away, people would speak of a Mixed Marriage. If a Philadelphian from Chestnut Hill married a . . . but he didn't.

–John Lukacs,

Philadelphia: Patricians and Philistines, 1900–1950, 1981

On the Streets

I walked the avenue till my legs felt like stone.
I heard the voices of friends vanished and gone.
At night I could hear the blood in my veins
Just as black and whispering as the rain
On the streets of Philadelphia.

—Bruce Springsteen,

"The Streets of Philadelphia," 1993

The Friendliest Metropolis

If you presume that big U.S. Cities are unfriendly places to visit, think again. A *Condé Naste Traveler* survey suggests that the country's major cities are getting a bum rap. Our reporters pounded the pavement in ten of them, conducting a dozen different tests in each. . . . The friendliest metropolis? Why, the City of Brotherly Love, of course. . . .

At Philadelphia's renowned French restaurant Le Bec-Fin, two tuxedoed staff members opened the door, and one said, "Sure, please," when our reporter asked to use the rest room.

–Gary Stoller,

"The Friendly Cities," 1994

Notes

Introduction

1. Anne Royall, *The Black Book: A Continuation of Travels in the United States* (Washington: Printed for the author, 1828), 1:96.

2. R. W. Emerson, *The Journals and Miscellaneous Notebooks of Ralph Waldo Emerson, 1841–1843*, ed. William H. Gilman and J. E. Parsons (Cambridge, Mass.: Harvard University Press, 1970), 8:334.

3. John Lukacs, *Philadelphia: Patricians and Philistines, 1900–1950* (New York: Farrar, Straus and Giroux, 1981).

4. Henry Caswall, *America, and the American Church* (London: Rivington, 1839), 157.

5. George Sessions Perry, *Cities of America* (New York: McGraw-Hill, 1947), 95–108.

Chapter 1: Mastering Philadelphia

1. Nikolai Gogol, *Diary of a Madman and Other Stories*, trans. Ronald Wilks (Baltimore: Penguin, 1974), 93.

2. Saul Bellow, *Mosby's Memoirs and Other Stories* (New York: Viking, 1968), 88–109.

3. Georg Simmel, "The Metropolis and Mental Life," in *The Sociology of Georg Simmel*, trans. and ed. Kurt H. Wolff (New York: Free Press, 1950), 409–24.

4. Morton and Lucia White in *The Intellectual Versus the City* (Cambridge, Mass.: Harvard University Press, 1962) discuss the three within a broad context of the city in American intellectual and imaginative life from the eighteenth century to the present time.

5. Thomas Hamilton, *Men and Manners in America* (Edinburgh: Blackwood, 1843), 192–93.

6. Lady Duffus Hardy, *Through Cities and Prairie Lands: Sketches of an American Tour* (New York: R. Worthington, 1881; reprint New York: Arno Press, 1974), 295–98.

7. James Dixon, *Personal Narrative of a Tour through a Part of the United States and Canada*, 2d ed. (New York: Lane and Scott, 1849), 51–52.

8. *The Quaker City; or, The Monks of Monk-Hall* (Philadelphia: Privately published, 1844), 3–4, 462.

9. The statistic suggests that the spacious, comfortable domestic life of Philadelphia seen by the traveler had its opposite, the crowded houses just out of sight. It should be noted that the statistic, in context, presents Philadelphia housing as being far less congested than that of other cities. New York had 16.36 occupants per dwelling in the later nineteenth century and the new city of Chicago, 8.24.

The standard source for the specific details of Philadelphia's growth is *Philadelphia: A 300-Year History*, ed. Russell Weigley (New York, Norton, 1982). The paragraph on housing density is on page 422. It draws upon the work of James F. Sutherland in his "Housing the Poor in the City of Homes: Philadelphia at the Turn of the Century" in *The Peoples of Philadelphia: A History of Ethnic Groups and Lower-Class Life, 1790–1940*, ed. Allen F. Davis and Mark A. Haller (Philadelphia: Temple University Press, 1973).

10. Alexis de Tocqueville, *Democracy in America*, trans. Henry Reeve, ed. Phillips Bradley, 2 vols. (New York: Knopf, 1963), 289–90.

11. William Chambers, *Things as They Are in America* (Philadelphia: Lippincott, Grambo, 1854), 304–22.

12. Frederick Marryat, *A Diary in America with Remarks on Its Institutions*, ed. Sydney Jackman (Westport, Conn.: Greenwood, 1973), 145–52.

13. Erving Goffman, *Relations in Public: Microstudies of the Public Order* (New York: Harper, 1972), 238–333.

14. Elizabeth Robins Pennell, *Our Philadelphia* (Philadelphia: Lippincott, 1914), 118–19. What the "rhyming list" rhymes with is "Market, Arch, Race, and Vine."

15. See, e.g., the essays on crime, violence, and housing in Davis and Haller, *The Peoples of Philadelphia* or Roger Lane, *Violent Death in the City: Suicide, Accident, and Murder in Nineteenth-Century Philadelphia* (Cambridge, Mass.: Harvard University Press, 1979).

16. The debate is well summarized by Thomas R. Winpenny in "The Nefarious Philadelphia Plan and Urban America: A Reconsideration," *PMHB* 101 (January 1977): 103–13.

17. Kevin Lynch, *The Image of the City* (Cambridge: MIT Press, 1960), 96–97.

18. William H. Whyte, *City: Rediscovering the Center* (New York: Doubleday, 1988), 318.

19. Charles Joseph Latrobe, *The Rambler in North America* (London: Seeley and Burnside, 1835), 27–28.

20. Anthony Trollope, *North America*, ed. Donald Smalley and Bradford Allen Booth (New York: Knopf, 1951), 291.

21. *Baggage and Boots; or Smith's First Peep at America* (London: Sunday School Union, 1883), 129.

22. Walt Whitman, *Prose Works 1892, Vol. I, Specimen Days*, ed. Floyd Stovall (New York: New York University Press, 1963), 189.

23. Henry James, *The American Scene* (New York: Scribner's, 1946), 273–302.

24. Ibid., 283–85.

25. Albert Camus, *American Journals*, trans. Hugh Levick (New York: Paragon House, 1987), 45.

Chapter 2: Walking Philadelphia

1. Jane Jacobs, *The Death and Life of Great American Cities* (New York: Knopf, 1961).

2. White, *City: Rediscovering the Center*, 206.

3. A. M. Maxwell, *A Run through the United States in the Autumn of 1840* (London: Colburn, 1841), 2:161–68.

4. Mrs. [Frances] Trollope, *Domestic Manners of the Americans* (Barre, Mass.: Imprint Society, 1969), 208.

5. John A. Lukacs, "A Hungarian Traveler in Pennsylvania," *PMHB* 73 (January 1949): 64–75.

6. Lynch, *The Image of the City*, 9 and passim.

7. Tyrone Power, *Impressions of America during the Years 1823, 1834, and 1835* (Philadelphia: Carey, Lea, and Blanchard, 1836), 54–61.

8. P. T. Barnum, *Struggles and Triumphs or Forty Years' Recollections* (Buffalo, N.Y.: Warren, Johnson, 1873), 264.

9. John F. Watson, *Annals of Philadelphia and Pennsylvania* (Philadelphia: Leary, Stuart, 1927), 230.

10. Richard L. Bushman, *The Refinement of America: Persons, Houses, Cities* (New York: Knopf, 1992), 354–63.

11. Sir Charles Lyell, *A Second Visit to the United States of North America* (New York: Harper, 1849), 241.

12. Frances Anne Butler [Kemble], *Journal* (London: John Murray, 1835), 1:174.

13. Charles Henry White, "Philadelphia," *Harper's Monthly Magazine* 113 (June 1906): 45.

14. Edward Hungerford, *The Personality of American Cities* (New York: McBride, Nast, 1913), 76–94.

15. George Barton, *Little Journeys around Old Philadelphia* (Philadelphia: Peter Reilly, 1926), 18–20.

16. Christopher Morley, *Christopher Morley's Philadelphia*, ed. Ken Kalfus (New York: Fordham University Press, 1990), 3–6.

17. Bill Bryson, *The Lost Continent: Travels in Small-Town America* (New York: Harper and Row, 1989), 126–30.

Chapter 3: Mythic Places

1. John F. Sears writes perceptively on the vogue, the motives, and the extent of asylums as tourist attractions in *Sacred Places* (New York: Oxford University Press, 1989), 89 ff.

2. Caroline Gilman, *The Poetry of Travelling in the United States with Additional Sketches by a Few Friends* (New York: Colman, 1838), 35–36.

3. Harriet Martineau, *Society in America* (London: Saunders and Otley, 1837; New York: AMS, 1966), 1:194–95.

4. Emily Faithfull, *Three Visits to America* (New York: Fowler and Wells, 1884), 87.

5. James F. W. Johnson, *Notes on North America* (Edinburgh: Blackwood, 1851), 2:304.

6. Chambers, *Things as They Are in America*, 307.

7. Trollope, *North America*, 291–92.

8. See Dennis C. Kurjack, "Evolution of a Shrine," *Pennsylvania History* 21 (July 1954): 193–200. For a remarkably rich description of the fortunes of Independence Hall and its surrounding buildings, see the series of four essays by Lewis Mumford titled "Historical Philadelphia," originally published in the *New Yorker* and later reprinted in *The Highway and the City* (New York: Harcourt, Brace and World, 1963). The definitive recent treatment of the subject is Constance M. Greiff's *Independence: The Creation of a National Park* (Philadelphia: University of Pennsylvania Press, 1987).

9. Captain Basil Hall, *Travels in North America in the Years 1827 and 1828* (Edinburgh: Cadell, 1829), 2:375–76.

10. R. A. Smith, *Philadelphia as It Is in 1852* (Philadelphia: Lindsay and Blakiston, 1852), 23–24.

11. Sears, *Sacred Places*, 3.

12. Dean MacCannell, *The Tourist: A New Theory of the Leisure Class* (New York: Schocken, 1976), 43–45.

13. Frederick Lewis, "Philadelphia," *Women's Home Companion* 54 (May 1927): 93.

14. James, *The American Scene*, 288–94.

15. The essential details of the history of the Liberty Bell are contained in a tart essay in the Mencken mode by Henry J. Ford: "The Liberty Bell," in *Readings from the American Mercury*, ed. Grant C. Knight (New York: Knopf, 1926). The most accessible account is contained in the booklet published by the National Park Service: David Kimball, *The Story of the Liberty Bell* (Philadelphia: Eastern National Park and Monument Association, 1989).

16. MacCannell, *The Tourist*, 137–40.

17. Michael Kammen, *Mystic Chords of Memory: The Transformation of Tradition in American Culture* (New York: Knopf, 1991), 52–56.

Chapter 4: The Great Granite Experiment

1. Hall, *Travels in North America*, 2:344–55.

2. The best account of the background, the concept, the execution, and the international reputation of the penitentiary is Norman Johnston, Kenneth Finkel, and Jeffrey Cohen, *Eastern State Penitentiary: Crucible of Good Intentions* (Philadelphia: Philadelphia Museum of Art, 1994).

3. Adam J. Hirsch, *The Rise of the Penitentiary: Prisons and Punishment in Early America* (New Haven, Conn.: Yale University Press, 1992).

4. Negley K. Teeters and John D. Shearer, *The Prison at Philadelphia,*

Cherry Hill: The Separate System of Penal Discipline, 1829–1913 (New York: Columbia University Press, 1957), 205.

5. For a full account, see Sears, *Sacred Places.*

6. Ibid., 98–99.

7. Hamilton, *Men and Manners in America,* 198.

8. George Wilson Pierson, *Tocqueville and Beaumont in America* (New York: Oxford University Press, 1938), 463.

9. Lieutenant Colonel Camille Ferri Pisani, *Prince Napoleon in America, 1861, Letters from His Aide-de-Camp,* trans. Georges J. Joyaux (Bloomington: Indiana University Press, 1959), 86.

10. Gilman, *The Poetry of Travelling,* 48.

11. Harriet Martineau, *Retrospective of Western Travel* (London: Saunders and Otley, 1838), 1:128.

12. Ibid., 132.

13. Chambers, *Things as They Are in America,* 308–11.

14. Quoted in Teeters and Shearer, *The Prison at Philadelphia,* 114.

15. Charles Dickens, *American Notes and Pictures from Italy* (London: Oxford University Press, 1957), 99.

16. Ibid., 101–2.

17. *Eleventh Annual Report of the Inspectors of the Eastern State Penitentiary of Pennsylvania* (Philadelphia: Brown, Bicking, and Guilbert, 1840), 13.

18. Teeters and Shearer, *The Prison at Philadelphia,* 113–32.

19. Gilman, *The Poetry of Travelling,* 49.

20. Thomas Brothers, *The United States of America as They Are: Not as They Are Generally Described: Being A Cure for Radicalism* (London: Longman, 1840), 20–32.

21. John Robert Godley, *Letters from America* (London: John Murray, 1844), 2:159–60.

22. Pierson, *Tocqueville and Beaumont,* 473.

23. Smith, *Philadelphia as It Is in 1852,* 385.

24. Jacqueline Thibaut gives an account of some of the ways in which the system had begun to unravel as early as the mid-1830s in "'To Pave the Way to Penitence': Prisoners and Discipline at the Eastern State Penitentiary, 1829–1835," *PMHB* 106 (April 1982): 187–222.

25. See Sears, *Sacred Places,* 99.

26. Theodore Dreiser, *The Financier* (Cleveland: World, n.d.), 427.

Chapter 5: Public Utility as Theme Park

1. Gilman, *The Poetry of Travelling,* 31–32.

2. Catherine L. Brooke, "Fairmount," *Godey's Lady's Book* 21 (September 1840): 142.

3. Mrs. Bromley, *A Woman's Wanderings in the Western World* (London: Saunders, Otley, 1861), 33.

4. John W. Oldmixon, *Transatlantic Wanderings: Or, A Last Look at the United States* (London: Routledge, 1855), 52.

5. W. E. Baxter, *America and the Americans* (London: Routledge, 1855), 28.

6. [Kemble], *Journal*, 1:195.

7. Dickens, *American Notes*, 98.

8. Smith, *Philadelphia as It Is in 1852*, 46.

9. J. Thomas Scharf and Thompson Westcott, *History of Philadelphia, 1609–1884* (Philadelphia: L. H. Everts, 1884), 3:1853.

10. Maxwell, *A Run through the United States*, 2:167.

11. Alfred Pairpoint, *Uncle Sam and His Country; or, Sketches of America in 1854–55–56* (London: Simpkin, Marshall, 1857), 302–3.

12. Mrs. [Francis] Trollope, *Domestic Manners of the Americans*, 205–6.

13. Sears, *Sacred Places*, 182. The classic treatment of the pastoral and the technological in American culture is Leo Marx, *The Machine in the Garden* (New York: Oxford University Press, 1964).

14. Jane M. E. Turnbull and Marion Turnbull, *American Photographs* (London: T. C. Newby, 1859), 2:164–65.

15. Charles Richard Weld, *A Vacation Tour in the United States and Canada* (London: Longman, Brown, Green, and Longmans, 1855), 356.

16. Simmel, in *The Sociology of Georg Simmel*, 409–24.

17. Michael Lesy, *Wisconsin Death Trip* (New York: Pantheon, 1973), n.p.

Chapter 6: Urban Woods

1. Edward Strahan, *A Century After: Picturesque Glimpses of Philadelphia and Pennsylvania* (Philadelphia: Allen, Lane, and Scott and J. W. Lauderbach, 1875), 7–8.

2. I. Finch, *Travels in the United States of America and Canada* (London: Longman, Rees, Orme, Brown, Green, and Longman, 1833), 74–78.

3. Charles Augustus Murray, *Travels in North America during the Years 1834, 1835, and 1836* (New York: Harper, 1839), 1:135–36.

4. Dixon, *Personal Narrative*, 50–51.

5. Henry D. Thoreau, *The Journal of Henry D. Thoreau*, ed. Bradford Torrey and Francis H. Allen (Boston: Houghton Mifflin, 1949), 7:72–74.

6. Lady Hardy, *Through Cities and Prairie Lands*, 301.

7. Frances Anne Butler [Kemble], *Journal*, 2:92–93.

8. A description of the exhibition was published as *A Walk on the Wild Side: The Wissahickon Creek, 1800–1940* ([Philadelphia]: The Library Company, [1993]).

9. Morley, *Christopher Morley's Philadelphia*, 219–20.

10. Elizabeth Bisland, *The Life and Letters of Lafcadio Hearn* (Boston: Houghton Mifflin, 1906), 469–70.

11. Jacques Offenbach, *Orpheus in America: Offenbach's Diary of His Journey to the New World* (Bloomington: Indiana University Press, 1957), 129–30.

12. Samuel Scoville Jr., "The Wildness of Philadelphia: How Nature Persists in a Metropolis," *Century* 3 (November 1925): 117–24.

13. Bryson, *The Lost Continent* (New York: Harper and Row, 1989), 126–30.

Chapter 7: American Athens

1. *Things as They Are; or, Notes of a Traveller* (New York: Harper, 1934), 29.

2. J. B., *The English Party's Excursion to Paris, in Easter Week 1849, to Which is Added a Trip to America* (London: Longman, 1850), 276.

3. Lukacs, "A Hungarian Traveler in Pennsylvania," 71.

4. B[enjamin] Henry Latrobe, *Anniversary Oration Pronounced before the Society of Artists of the United States* (Philadelphia: Bradford and Inskeep, 1811), 17.

5. Mrs. Basil Hall, *The Aristocratic Journey*, ed. Una Pope-Hennessy (New York: Putnam, 1931), 134–52.

6. Faithfull, *Three Visits to America*, 86–98.

7. Captain Basil Hall, *Travels in North America*, 2:366.

8. Travelers, of course, saw only a fraction of the intellectual energy of the first half of the nineteenth century. Edgar P. Richardson's chapter "The Athens of America: 1800–1825" in *Philadelphia: A 300-Year History*, ed. Russell F. Weigley (New York: Norton, 1982), remarks on the brilliance of various figures in the natural sciences during the period. "The fact that so many of these men working in Philadelphia have been honored as the 'father' of one or another American science gives testimony to the intellectual creativity their milieu engendered" (p. 242).

9. Achille Murat, *A Moral and Political Sketch of the United States of North America* (London: Effingham Wilson, 1833), 351–52.

10. William Bennett Banks, "Picturesque Philadelphia," *Munsey's Magazine* 6 (December 1891): 260.

11. Lieutenant Colonel Arthur Cunynghame, *A Glimpse at the Great Western Republic* (London: Richard Bentley, 1851), 293–95.

12. Marryat, *A Diary in America with Remarks on Its Institutions*, 147; and Oldmixon, *Transatlantic Wanderings*, 44.

13. William Ferguson, *America by River and Rail* (London: J. Nisbet, 1856), 203.

14. Sir Edward W. Watkin, *A Trip to the United States and Canada* (London: W. H. Smith, 1852), 98.

15. Chambers, *Things as They Are in America*, 313.

16. Cunynghame, *A Glimpse at the Great Western Republic*, 295.

17. Hungerford, *The Personality of American Cities*, 88.

18. Richard Cobden, *The American Diaries of Richard Cobden*, ed. Elizabeth H. Cawley (New York: Greenwood, 1969), 176.

19. Dickens, *American Notes*, 99.

20. Hamilton, *Men and Manners in America*, 194–95.

21. Hall, *Travels in North America*, 2:338–75.

22. For an excellent description, see Anne H. Wharton, "The Philadelphia Wistar Parties," *Lippincott's Magazine* 39 (June 1887): 978–88.

23. Shane Leslie, *American Wonderland: Memories of Four Tours in the United States of America (1911–1935)* (London: Michael Joseph, 1936), 109–20.

24. Ethel A. Starbird, "They'd Rather Be in Philadelphia," *National Geographic* 163 (March 1983): 314–43.

Chapter 8: Loathing Philadelphia

1. Paul F. Boller Jr. and John George, *They Never Said It: A Book of Fake Quotes, Misquotes, and Misleading Attributions* (New York: Oxford University Press, 1989), 26.

2. Sidney George Fisher, *A Philadelphia Perspective: The Diary of Sidney George Fisher*, ed. Nicholas B. Wainwright (Philadelphia: Historical Society of Pennsylvania, 1967), 134.

3. Ibid., 528.

4. Ellis Paxson Oberholtzer, *The Literary History of Philadelphia* (Philadelphia: Jacobs, 1906), xi.

5. Matthew Arnold, *Letters of Matthew Arnold, 1848–1888*, ed. George W. E. Russell (New York: Macmillan, 1895), 2:291.

6. Emily Toth, *Kate Chopin* (New York: William Morrow, 1990), 102.

7. An engaging account of the entire episode is contained in Barton, *Little Journeys around Old Philadelphia*, 296–306.

8. Philip Gibbs, *People of Destiny: Americans as I Saw Them at Home and Abroad* (New York: Harper, 1920), 58.

9. White, "Philadelphia," 42.

10. William Archer, *America To-Day: Observations and Reflections* (reprint of 1899 edition, New York: Arno Press, 1974), 36.

11. Pennell, *Our Philadelphia*, 19.

12. Edwin Wolf II, "The Origins of Philadelphia's Self-Depreciation, 1820–1920," *PMHB* 104 (January 1980): 58–73.

13. Beatrice Webb, *American Diary, 1898*, ed. David A. Shannon (Madison: University of Wisconsin Press, 1963), 44–45.

14. Lincoln Steffens, "Philadelphia: Corrupt and Contented," *McClure's* 21 (July 1903): 249–63.

15. Michael P. McCarthy explores the negative image of the city in "The Unprogressive City: Philadelphia and Urban Stereotypes at the Turn of the Century," *Pennsylvania History* 54 (October 1987): 263–81.

16. Alan Frazier, "Philadelphia: City of Brotherly Loot," *American Mercury* 47 (July 1939): 275–82.

17. Michael Middleton, *Man Made the Town* (New York: St. Martin's, 1987), 14.

18. Eugene Richards, "Philadelphia," *Granta* 38 (Winter 1991): 173–93.

19. Jonathan Yardley, *States of Mind: A Personal Journey through the Mid-Atlantic* (New York: Villard, 1993), 30.

Chapter 9: Dreaming Philadelphia

1. Edward Dicey, *Six Months in The Federal States* (London: Macmillan, 1863), 1:53–55.

2. Harry Emerson Wildes, *William Penn* (New York: Macmillan, 1974), 138.

3. Gillian Roberts, *Caught Dead in Philadelphia* (New York: Ballantine, 1987), 119.

4. Ford Madox Ford, *The Good Soldier* (New York: Vintage, 1955), 153–54.

5. Peter Handke, "Short Letter, Long Farewell" in *Three by Peter Handke* (New York: Avon, 1977), 136–37.

6. T. Coraghessan Boyle, *East Is East* (New York: Viking, 1990).

Bibliography

Adams, Charles Francis. *Diaries*. Ed. Marc Friedlander and L. H. Butterfield. 6 vols. Cambridge: Harvard University Press, 1964–74.

Alexander, J. E. *Transatlantic Sketches, Comprising Visits to the Most Interesting Scenes in North and South America*. Philadelphia: Key and Biddle, 1833.

Alpert, Hollis. "Philadelphia: Plans and Pigeons." *Partisan Review* 17 (September–October 1950): 697–706.

Archer, William. *America To-Day: Observations and Reflections*. 1899. Reprint, New York: Arno Press, 1974.

Arnold, Matthew. *Letters of Matthew Arnold, 1848–1888*. Ed. George W. E. Russell. 2 vols. New York: Macmillan, 1895.

Aubertin, J. J. *A Fight with Distances*. London: Kegan Paul, 1888.

Baedeker, Karl, ed. *The United States with an Excursion into Mexico: Handbook for Travellers*. Leipsic: Karl Baedeker, 1893.

Baggage and Boots; or, Smith's First Peep at America. London: Sunday School Union, 1883.

Baltzell, E. Digby. *Puritan Boston and Quaker Philadelphia*. Boston: Beacon, 1979.

Banks, William Bennett. "Picturesque Philadelphia." *Munsey's Magazine* 6 (December 1891): 251–363.

Barnes, Harry Elmer. *The Evolution of Penology in Pennsylvania*. 1927. Reprint, Montclair, N.J.: Patterson Smith, 1968.

Barnum, P. T. *Struggles and Triumphs or Forty Years' Recollections*. Buffalo: Warren, Johnson, 1813.

Barton, George. *Little Journeys around Old Philadelphia*. Philadelphia: Peter Reilly, 1926.

Baxter, W. E. *America and the Americans*. London: Routledge, 1855.

Bellow, Saul. *Mosby's Memoirs and Other Stories*. New York: Viking, 1968.

Berry, C. B. *The Other Side and How It Struck Us*. London: Griffith and Farran, 1880.

Bingham, Katharine. *The Philadelphians as Seen by a New York Woman*. Boston: L. C. Page, 1903.

Bisland, Elizabeth. *The Life and Letters of Lafcadio Hearn*. 2 vols. Boston: Houghton Mifflin, 1906.

[Blane, William Newnham]. *Travels through the United States and Canada*. London: Baldwin and Co., 1828.

Boller, Paul F. Jr., and John George. *They Never Said It: A Book of Fake Quotes, Misquotes, and Misleading Attributions*. New York: Oxford University Press, 1989.

Boyle, T. Coraghessan. *East Is East*. New York: Viking, 1990.

Brand, Dana. *The Spectator and the City in Nineteenth-Century American Literature*. New York: Cambridge University Press, 1991.

Brandow, James C. "A Barbadoes Planter's Visit to Philadelphia in 1837: The
Journal of Nathaniel T. W. Carrington." *PMHB* 106 (July 1982): 411–21.

[Bremer, Frederika]. *America in the Fifties: Letters of Frederika Bremer*. Selected
and edited by Adolph B. Benson. New York: American-Scandinavian Foun-
dation, 1924.

Bright, Henry Arthur. *Happy Country This America: The Travel Diaries of Henry
Arthur Bright*. Ed. Anne Henry Ehrenpreis. Columbus: Ohio State University Press, 1978.

Bromley, Mrs. *A Woman's Wanderings in the Western World*. London: Saunders,
Otley, 1861.

Brooke, Catherine L. "Fairmount." *Godey's Lady's Book* 21 (September 1840):
142.

Brothers, Thomas. *The United States of North America as They Are; Not as They
Are Generally Described: Being A Cure For Radicalism*. London: Longman,
1840.

Bruce, Edward V. "Philadelphia's Hotel-De-Ville." *Lippincott's Magazine* 33 (January 1884): 8–23.

Bryant, William Cullen. *Picturesque America*. 2 vols. New York: Appleton, 1872.

Bryce, James. *The American Commonwealth*. 2 vols. New York: Macmillan, 1895.

Bryson, Bill. *The Lost Continent: Travels in Small-Town America*. New York: Harper and Row, 1989.

Buckingham, J. S. *America: Historical, Statistic, and Descriptive*. 2 vols. New
York: Harper, 1841.

Burt, Nathaniel. *The Perennial Philadelphians: The Anatomy of an American Aristocracy*. Boston: Little Brown, 1963.

Bushman, Richard L. *The Refinement of America: Persons, Houses, Cities*. New
York: Knopf, 1992.

Butor, Michel. "Travel and Writing," *Mosaic* 8 (Fall 1974): 1–16.

Cameron, William. *A Month in the United States and Canada*. Edinburgh: Men-
zies, 1873.

Camus, Albert. *American Journals*. Trans. Hugh Levick. New York: Paragon
House, 1987.

[Candler, Isaac]. *A Summary View of America by an Englishman*. London: T. Cadell, 1824.

Carlisle, Marcia. "Disorderly City, Disorderly Women," *PMHB* 110 (October
1986): 549–68.

Caswall, Henry. *America, and the American Church*. London: Rivington, 1839.

Chadwick, Philip, and Foster Smith. *Philadelphia on the River*. Philadelphia:
Philadelphia Maritime Museum, 1988.

Chambers, William. *Things as They Are in America*. Philadelphia: Lippincott,
Grambo, 1854.

Chesterton, G. K. *What I Saw in America*. 1922. Reprint, New York: Da Capo
Press, 1968.

Clay, Grady. *Close-Up: How to Read the American City.* New York: Praeger, 1973.

Cobbett, William. *A Year's Residence in the United States of America.* New York: Augustus M. Kelley, 1869.

Cobden, Richard. *The American Diaries of Richard Cobden.* Ed. Elizabeth H. Cawley. New York: Greenwood, 1969.

Cole, Garold L. *Travels in America: From the Voyages of Discovery to the Present. An Annotated Bibliography of Travel Articles in Periodicals, 1955–1980.* Norman: University of Oklahoma Press, 1984.

Combe, George. *Notes on the United States of North America during a Phrenological Visit in 1838–9–40.* 3 vols. Philadelphia: Carey and Hall, 1841.

Conrad, Peter. *Imagining America.* New York: Oxford University Press, 1980.

Cunynghame, Arthur. *A Glimpse at the Great Western Republic.* London: Richard Bentley, 1851.

Daly, T. A. *The Wissahickon.* Philadelphia: Garden Club of Philadelphia, 1922.

[D'Arusment, Frances Wright]. *Views of Society and Manners in America.* London: Longman, Hurst, 1821.

Davis, Allen F., and Mark H. Haller, eds. *The Peoples of Philadelphia: A History of Ethnic Groups and Lower-Class Life, 1790–1940.* Philadelphia: Temple University Press, 1973.

Davis, Rebecca Harding. "A Glimpse of Philadelphia in July, 1776." *Lippincott's Magazine* 18 (July 1876): 27–38.

———. "Old Philadelphia." *Harper's Monthly* 52 (April 1876): 705–21; (May 1876): 868–82.

Day, Samuel Phillips. *Life and Society in America.* London: Newman, 1880.

de Bacourt, [Adolphe Fouvier]. *Souvenirs of a Diplomat.* New York: Henry Holt, 1885.

DeBeauvoir, Simone. *America Day by Day.* New York: Grove, 1953.

[Decon, Thomas William]. *The Experiences of an Englishman in Philadelphia Society.* Philadelphia: N.p., c. 1887.

Deshler, Charles D. "How the Declaration Was Received in the Old Thirteen." *Harper's Monthly* 85 (July 1892): 165–87.

D'Estounelles de Constant, Paul H. *America and Her Problems.* New York: Macmillan, 1915.

Dexter, Pete. *Brotherly Love.* New York: Random House, 1991.

———. *God's Pocket.* New York: Random House, 1983.

Dicey, Edward. *Six Months in the Federal States.* 2 vols. London: Macmillan, 1863.

Dickens, Charles. *American Notes and Pictures from Italy.* London: Oxford University Press, 1957.

Dixon, James. *Personal Narrative of a Tour through a Part of the United States and Canada.* 2d ed. New York: Lane and Scott, 1849.

Dreiser, Theodore. *The Financier.* Cleveland: World, n.d.

Driver, Clive E., ed. *Passing Through: Letters and Documents Written in Philadelphia by Famous Visitors.* Philadelphia: Rosenbach Museum, 1982.

DuBois, W. E. B. *The Philadelphia Negro.* Millwood, N.Y.: Kraus-Thomson, 1973.

Duncan, John M. *Travels through Part of the United States and Canada in 1818 and 1819.* New York: W. B. Gilley, 1823.

Eighth Annual Report of the Inspectors of the Eastern State Penitentiary of Pennsylvania. Philadelphia: J. Thomson, 1837.

Eleventh Annual Report of the Inspectors of the Eastern State Penitentiary of Pennsylvania. Philadelphia: Brown, Bicking, and Guilbert, 1840.

Emerson, R. W. *The Journals and Miscellaneous Notebooks of Ralph Waldo Emerson, 1841–1843.* Vol. 8. Ed. William H. Gilman and J. E. Parsons. Cambridge, Mass.: Harvard University Press, 1970.

Faithfull, Emily. *Three Visits to America.* New York: Fowler and Wells, 1884.

Fearon, Henry Bradshaw. *Sketches of America: A Narrative of a Journey.* London: Longman, Hurst, Rees, Orme, and Brown, 1818.

Ferguson, William. *America by River and Rail.* London: J. Nisbet, 1856.

Fifty-fourth Annual Report of the Inspectors of the State Penitentiary for the Eastern District of Pennsylvania. Philadelphia: Allen, Lane and Scott, 1884.

Finch, I. *Travels in the United States of America and Canada.* London: Longman, Rees, Orme, Brown, Green, and Longman, 1833.

Finkel, Kenneth, ed. *Philadelphia Almanac and Citizens' Manual for 1994.* Philadelphia: Library Company, 1994.

Finkel, Kenneth, and Susan Oyama. *Philadelphia Then and Now.* New York: Dover, 1988.

First and Second Annual Reports of the Inspectors of the Eastern State Penitentiary of Pennsylvania. Philadelphia: Thomas Kite, 1831.

Fisher, Sidney George. *A Philadelphia Perspective: The Diary of Sidney George Fisher.* Ed. Nicholas B. Wainwright. Philadelphia: Historical Society of Pennsylvania, 1967.

[Flint, James]. *Flint's Letters from America, 1818–1820.* Ed. Reuben Gold Thwaits. Vol. 9. *Early Western Travel, 1748–1846.* Cleveland, Ohio: Arthur H. Clark, 1964.

Ford, Ford Madox. *The Good Soldier.* New York: Vintage, 1955.

Ford, Henry J. "The Liberty Bell." In *Readings from the American Mercury,* ed. Grant C. Knight. New York: Knopf, 1926.

Frazier, Alan. "Philadelphia: City of Brotherly Loot." *American Mercury* 47 (July 1939): 275–82.

Gibbs, Philip. *People of Destiny: Americans as I Saw Them at Home and Abroad.* New York: Harper, 1920.

Gillespie, Dizzy, with Al Fraser. *To Be, or Not . . . to Bop.* Garden City, N.Y.: Doubleday, 1979.

Gilman, Caroline. *The Poetry of Travelling in the United States with Additional Sketches by a Few Friends.* New York: S. Colman, 1838.

Glazier, Willard. *Peculiarities of American Cities.* Philadelphia: Hubbard, 1886.

Godley, John Robert. *Letters from America.* 2 vols. London: John Murray, 1844.

Goffman, Erving. *Relations in Public: Microstudies of the Public Order.* New York: Harper, 1972.

Gogol, Nikolai. *Diary of a Madman and Other Stories.* Trans. Ronald Wilks. Baltimore: Penguin, 1974.

Grattan, Thomas Collet. *Civilized America,* 2d ed. 2 vols. London: Bradbury and Evans, 1859.

Greiff, Constance M. *Independence: The Creation of a National Park.* Philadelphia: University of Pennsylvania Press, 1987.

Gripenberg, Alexandra. *A Half Year in the New World.* Trans. and ed. Ernest J. Moyne. Newark: University of Delaware Press, 1954.

Gunther, John. *Inside U.S.A.* Revised ed. New York: Harper and Row, 1951.

Hall, Basil. *Travels in North America in the Years 1827 and 1828.* 3 vols. Edinburgh: Cadell, 1829.

Hall, Mrs. Basil. *The Aristocratic Journey.* [1827.] Ed. Una Pope-Hennessy. New York: Putnam, 1931.

Hall, Francis. *Travels in Canada and the United States in 1816 and 1817.* London: Longman, Hurst, Rees, Orme, and Brown, 1818.

Hamilton, Thomas. *Men and Manners in America.* Edinburgh: Blackwood, 1843.

Hamy, E.-T. *The Travels of a Naturalist: Charles A. Lesueur in North America, 1815–1837.* Trans. Nilton Haber. Ed. H. F. Raup. Kent, Ohio: Kent State University Press, 1968.

Handke, Peter. "Short Letter, Long Farewell." In *Three by Peter Handke.* New York: Avon, 1977.

Hardy, Lady Duffus. *Through Cities and Prairie Lands: Sketches of an American Tour.* New York: R. Worthington, 1881. Reprint, New York: Arno Press, 1974.

Hirsch, Adam J. *The Rise of the Penitentiary: Prisons and Punishment in Early America.* New Haven, Conn.: Yale University Press, 1992.

Hiss, Tony. *The Experience of Place.* New York: Knopf, 1990.

Hole, S. Reynolds. *A Little Tour in America.* Freeport, N.Y.: Books for Libraries Press, 1971.

Holyoake, George Jacob. *Among the Americans.* Chicago: Belford, Clarke, 1881.

Howe, Irving. "The City in Literature." *Commentary* 51 (May 1971): 61–68.

Howitt, E. *Selections from Letters Written during a Tour through the United States.* Nottingham: J. Dunn, [1820].

Hungerford, Edward. *The Personality of American Cities.* New York: McBride, Nast, 1913.

Jackson, Joseph. *Iconography of Philadelphia.* Philadelphia: Privately printed, 1934.

Jacobs, Harriet. *Incidents in the Life of a Slave Girl.* New York: Oxford University Press, 1988.

Jacobs, Jane. *The Death and Life of Great American Cities.* New York: Knopf, 1961.

James, Henry. *The American Scene.* New York: Scribner's, 1946.

Janson, Charles William. *The Stranger in America: 1793–1806.* Ed. Carl S. Driver. New York: Press of the Pioneers, 1935.

Jayne, Michael C., and Ann Chalmer Watts, eds. *Literature and the Urban Experience: Essays on the City and Literature.* New Brunswick, N.J.: Rutgers, 1981.

J. B. *The English Party's Excursion to Paris, in Easter Week 1849, to Which Is Added a Trip to America.* London: Longman, 1850.

Johnson, James F. W. *Notes on North America.* 2 vols. Edinburgh: Blackwood, 1851.

Johnston, Norman, Kenneth Finkel, and Jeffrey A. Cohen. *Eastern State Penitentiary: Crucible of Good Intentions.* Philadelphia: Philadelphia Museum of Art, 1994.

Kagle, Steven E., ed. *America: Exploration and Travel.* Bowling Green, Ohio: Bowling Green State University Popular Press, 1979.

Kammen, Michael. *Mystic Chords of Memory: The Transformation of Tradition in American Culture.* New York: Knopf, 1991.

[Kemble], Frances Anne Butler. *Journal.* 2 vols. London: John Murray, 1835.

Keyser, Charles S. *Fairmount Park: Sketches of Its Scenery, Waters, and History.* 5th ed. Philadelphia: Claxton, Remsen, and Haffelfinger, 1872.

Kimball, David. *The Story of the Liberty Bell.* Philadelphia: Eastern National Park and Monument Association, 1989.

Kipling, Rudyard. "Philadelphia." In *Rewards and Fairies.* Garden City, N.Y.: Doubleday Page, 1920.

Kurjack, Dennis C. "Evolution of a Shrine." *Pennsylvania History* 21 (July 1954): 193–200.

Lakier, Aleksandr Borisovich. *A Russian Looks at America: The Journey of Aleksandr Borisovich Lakier.* Trans. and ed. Arnold Schrier and Joyce Story. Chicago: University of Chicago Press, 1979.

Lane, Christopher, and Donald H. Cresswell. *Prints of Philadelphia at the Philadelphia Print Shop.* Philadelphia: N.p., 1990.

Lane, Roger. *Violent Death in the City: Suicide, Accident, and Murder in Nineteenth-Century Philadelphia.* Cambridge, Mass.: Harvard University Press, 1979.

Latrobe, B[enjamin] Henry. *Anniversary Oration Pronounced before the Society of Artists of the United States.* Philadelphia: Bradford and Inskeep, 1811.

Latrobe, Charles Joseph. *The Rambler in North America.* London: Seeley and Burnside, 1835.

Latt, Jack, and Lee Mortimer. *USA Confidential.* New York: Crown, 1952.

Lattimore, Richmond. "Max Schmitt in a Single Scull." In *Poems from Three Decades.* New York: Scribner's, 1972.

Lees, Andrew. *Cities Perceived: Urban Society in European and American Thought, 1820–1940.* New York: Columbia University Press, 1985.

Leslie, Shane. *American Wonderland: Memories of Four Tours in the United States of America (1911–1935).* London: Michael Joseph, 1936.

Lesy, Michael. *Wisconsin Death Trip.* New York: Pantheon, 1973.

Lev, Micha. *Yordim.* N.p.: Woodbine House, 1988.

Lewis, Frederick. "Philadelphia." *Women's Home Companion* 54 (May 1927): 14+.

Lieber, Francis. *The Stranger in America.* Philadelphia: Carey, Lea, 1835.

Lingeman, Richard. *Theodore Dreiser: At the Gates of the City, 1871–1907.* New York: Putnam, 1986.

Lippard, George. *The Quaker City, or, The Monks of Monk-Hall.* Philadelphia: Privately printed, 1844.

Lloyd, Lewis, and Henry Justin Smith. *Oscar Wilde Discovers America.* New York: Harcourt, 1936.

Logan, James. *Notes of a Journey through Canada, the United States of America and the West Indies.* Edinburgh: Fraser, 1838.

Love, Nancy. *Greater Philadelphia Magazine's Guide to Philadelphia*. Philadelphia: Greater Philadelphia Magazine, 1965.

Lukacs, John A. "A Hungarian Traveler in Pennsylvania." *PMHB* 73 (January 1949): 64–75.

———. *Philadelphia: Patricians and Philistines, 1900–1950*. New York: Farrar, Straus and Giroux, 1981.

Lynch, Kevin. *The Image of the City*. Cambridge: MIT Press, 1960.

Lyell, Sir Charles. *A Second Visit to the United States of North America*. New York: Harper, 1849.

MacCannell, Dean. *The Tourist: A New Theory of the Leisure Class*. New York: Shocken, 1976.

Mackay, Alexander. "A British Traveler in Philadelphia." In *The Leaven of Democracy: The Growth of the Democratic Spirit in the Time of Jackson*, ed. Clement Eaton. New York: Braziller, 1963.

Marryat, Frederick. *A Diary in America with Remarks on Its Institutions*. Ed. Sydney Jackman. Westport, Conn.: Greenwood, 1973.

Martineau, Harriet. *Retrospect of Western Travel*. 2 vols. London: Saunders and Otley, 1838.

———. *Society in America*. 3 vols. London: Saunders and Otley, 1837; New York: AMS, 1966.

Marx, Leo. *The Machine in the Garden*. New York: Oxford University Press, 1964.

Maxwell, A. M. *A Run through the United States during the Autumn of 1840*. London: Colburn, 1841.

McCarthy, Michael P. "The Unprogressive City: Philadelphia and Urban Stereotypes at the Turn of the Century." *Pennsylvania History* 54 (October 1987): 263–81.

McHale, Tom. *Principato*. New York: Viking, 1970.

McKay, Claude. *Home to Harlem*. New York: Harper, 1928.

Middleton, Michael. *Man Made the Town*. New York: St. Martin's, 1987.

Miller, Alphonse B. "Philadelphia." *American Mercury* 9 (October 1926): 199–206.

Mohr, Niclaus. *Excursion through America*. Ed. Ray Allen Billington. Chicago: Lakeside Press, 1973.

Morley, Christopher. *Christopher Morley's Philadelphia*. Ed. Ken Kalfus. New York: Fordham University Press, 1990.

———. *Travels in Philadelphia*. Philadelphia: David McKay, 1921.

Muirhead, James Fullerton. *The Land of Contrasts*. Leipzig: Tauchnitz, 1900.

Mumford, Lewis. *The Highway and the City*. New York: Harcourt, Brace and World, 1963.

Murat, Achille. *A Moral and Political Sketch of the United States of North America*. London: Effingham Wilson, 1833.

Murray, Charles Augustus. *Travels in North America during the Years 1834, 1835, and 1836*. New York: Harper, 1839.

Oberholtzer, Ellis Paxson. *The Literary History of Philadelphia*. Philadelphia: Jacobs, 1906.

————. *Philadelphia: A History of the City and Its People*. 4 vols. Philadelphia: Clarke, 1911.

Offenbach, Jacques. *Orpheus in America: Offenbach's Diary of His Journey to the New World*. [1876] Bloomington: Indiana University Press, 1957.

Oldmixon, Captain [John W.]. *Transatlantic Wanderings: Or, A Last Look at the United States*. London: Routledge, 1855.

Pairpoint, Alfred. *Uncle Sam and His Country; or, Sketches of America in 1854–55–56*. London: Simpkin, Marshall, 1857.

Pennell, Elizabeth Robins. *Our Philadelphia*. Philadelphia: Lippincott, 1914.

Perelman, S. J. *Westward Ha!, or, Around the World in Eighty Clichés*. New York: Simon and Schuster, 1948.

Perry, George Sessions. "Philadelphia." In *Cities of America*. New York: McGraw-Hill, 1947.

Pierson, George Wilson. *Tocqueville and Beaumont in America*. New York: Oxford University Press, 1938.

Pisani, Camille Ferri. *Prince Napoleon in America, 1861, Letters from His Aide-de-Camp*. Trans. Georges J. Joyaux. Bloomington: Indiana University Press, 1959.

Pizer, Donald. *The Novels of Theodore Dreiser*. Minneapolis: University of Minnesota Press, 1976.

Poe, Edgar Allan. "Morning on the Wissahickon." In *The Opal: A Pure Gift for the Holy Days*. New York: John C. Riker, 1844.

Porter, Thomas. *Picture of Philadelphia from 1811 to 1831*. Philadelphia: Robert Desilver, 1831.

Posner, Russell M. "Philadelphia in 1830: An English View." *PMHB* 95 (April 1971): 239–43.

Power, Tyrone. *Impressions of America during the Years 1833, 1834, and 1835*. 2 vols. Philadelphia: Carey, Lea, and Blanchard, 1836.

Prentice, Archibald. *A Tour in the United States*. London: Johnson, 1848.

Pulszky, Francis, and Theresa Pulszky. *White, Red, Black: Sketches of American Society in the United States*. 2 vols. New York: Redfield, 1853.

Ratzel, Fredrick. "Philadelphia on the Eve of the Nation's Centennial: A Visitor's Description in 1873–74." Trans. and ed. Stewart A. Stehlin. *Pennsylvania History* 44 (January 1977): 25–36.

Reps, John W. *The Making of Urban America: A History of City Planning in the United States*. Princeton, N.J.: Princeton University Press, 1965.

Review of *A Century After: Picturesque Glimpses of Philadelphia and Pennsylvania. Lippincott's Magazine* 16 (December 1875): 775–76.

Richards, Eugene. "Philadelphia." *Granta* 38 (Winter 1991): 173–93.

Roberts, Gillian. *Caught Dead in Philadelphia*. New York: Ballantine, 1987.

Rosewater, Victor. *The Liberty Bell: Its History and Significance*. New York: Appleton, 1926.

Royall, Anne. *The Black Book; A Continuation of Travels in the United States*. 2 vols. Washington: Printed for the author, 1828.

————. *Sketches of History: Life and Manners in the United States by a Traveller*. New Haven, Conn.: Printed for the author, 1826.

[Sarmiento, Domingo]. *Sarmiento's Travels in the United States in 1847*. Trans. Michael A. Rockland. Princeton, N.J.: Princeton University Press, 1970.

Scharf, J. Thomas, and Thompson Westcott. *History of Philadelphia, 1609–1884*. 3 vols. Philadelphia: L. H. Everts, 1884.

Schurz, Karl. *The Reminiscences of Karl Schurz*. New York: McClure, 1907.

Scoville, Samuel Jr. "The Wildness of Philadelphia: How Nature Persists in a Metropolis." *Century* 3 (November 1925): 117–24.

Sears, John F. *Sacred Places*. New York: Oxford University Press, 1989.

Sherman, Constance D. "A French Artist Describes Philadelphia." *PMHB* 82 (April 1958): 204–15.

Sigourney, L[ydia] H. *Scenes in My Native Land*. Boston: James Munroe, 1845.

Simmel, Georg. "The Metropolis and Mental Life." In *The Sociology of Georg Simmel*. Trans. and ed. Kurt H. Wolff. New York: Free Press, 1950.

Sleigh, Lieutenant Colonel [Adderley W.]. *Pine Forests and Hacmatack Clearings; or Travel, Life, and Adventure, in the British North American Provinces*. London: Richard Bentley, 1853.

Smith, R. A. *Philadelphia as It Is in 1852*. Philadelphia: Lindsay and Blakiston, 1852.

Snyder, Martin P. "William Birch: His Philadelphia Views." *PMHB* 72 (July 1949): 271–315.

Solmssen, Arthur R. G. *Rittenhouse Square*. Boston: Little Brown, 1968.

Springsteen, Bruce. *Streets of Philadelphia*. Miami, Fla.: C. C. P. Belwin, 1993.

Starbird, Ethel A. "They'd Rather Be in Philadelphia." *National Geographic* 163 (March 1983): 314–43.

Steen, Ivan D. "Philadelphia in the 1850's as Described by British Travelers." *Pennsylvania History* 33 (January 1966): 30–49.

Steevens, G. W. *The Land of the Dollar*. Edinburgh: William Blackwood, 1897.

Steffens, Lincoln. *The Autobiography of Lincoln Steffens*. New York: Harcourt, 1931.

———. "Philadelphia: Corrupt and Contented." *McClure's* 21 (July 1903): 249–63.

[Stockton, Louise, ed.]. *A Sylvan City: or, Quaint Corners in Philadelphia*. Philadelphia: Our Continent Publishing Co., 1885.

Stoller, Gary. "The Friendly Cities." *Condé Nast Traveler* (September 1994): 25–28.

Strahan, Edward [Earl Shinn]. *A Century After: Picturesque Glimpses of Philadelphia and Pennsylvania*. Philadelphia: Allen, Lane, Scott, and J. W. Lauderbach, 1875.

Stuart, James. *Three Years in North America*. 2 vols. Edinburgh: Cadell, 1833.

Sturge, Joseph. *A Visit to the United States in 1841*. London: Hamilton, Adams and Co., 1842.

Sutcliff, Robert. *Travels in Some Parts of North America in the Years 1804, 1805, and 1806*. Philadelphia: B. and T. Kite, 1812.

Tanner, H. S. *The American Traveller; or Guide through the United States*. 3d ed. Philadelphia: Published by the author, 1837.

Taylor, George Rogers. "'Philadelphia in Slices' by George G. Foster." *PMHB* 93 (January 1969): 23–72.

Teeters, Negley K., and John D. Shearer. *The Prison at Philadelphia, Cherry Hill: The Separate System of Penal Discipline, 1829–1913*. New York: Columbia University Press, 1957.

Thibaut, Jacqueline. "'To Pave the Way to Penitence': Prisoners and Discipline at the Eastern State Penitentiary, 1829–1835." *PMHB* 106 (April 1982): 187–222.

Things as They Are; or, Notes of a Traveller. New York: Harper, 1834.

Thoreau, Henry D. *The Journal of Henry D. Thoreau*. Ed. Bradford Torrey and Francis H. Allen. 14 vols. Boston: Houghton Mifflin, 1949.

Tinkcom, Harry M. "Sir Augustus in Pennsylvania: The Travels and Observations of Sir Augustus J. Foster in Early Nineteenth-Century Pennsylvania." *PMHB* 75 (October 1951): 369–99.

Tocqueville, Alexis de. *Democracy in America*. Trans. Henry Reeve. Ed. Phillips Bradley. 2 vols. New York: Knopf, 1963.

Toth, Emily. *Kate Chopin*. New York: William Morrow, 1990.

Trachtenberg, Alan. "The American Scene: Versions of the City." *Massachusetts Review* 8 (Spring 1967): 281–95.

Trautmann, Frederick. "Pennsylvania through a German's Eyes: The Travels of Ludwig Gall, 1819–1820." *PMHB* 105 (January 1981): 35–65.

———. "Philadelphia Bowled Clean Over: Public Readings by Charles Dickens." *PMHB* 98 (October 1974): 456–68.

Trollope, Anthony. *North America*. Ed. Donald Smalley and Bradford Allen Booth. New York: Knopf, 1951.

Trollope, Mrs. [Francis]. *Domestic Manners of the Americans*. Barre, Mass.: Imprint Society, 1969.

Tudor, Henry. *Narrative of a Tour in North America*. 2 vols. London: James Duncan, 1834.

Turnbull, Jane M. E., and Marion Turnbull. *American Photographs*. 2 vols. London: T. C. Newby, 1859.

Twain, Mark. Untitled letter. In *Passing Through: Letters and Documents Written in Philadelphia by Famous Visitors*. Ed. Clive E. Driver. Philadelphia: Rosenbach Museum and Library, 1982.

Twelfth Annual Report of the Inspectors of the Eastern State Penitentiary of Pennsylvania. Philadelphia: E. G. Dorsey, 1841.

Wagner, Charles. *My Impressions of America*. New York: McClure, Phillips and Co., 1906.

Wainwright, Nicholas B. *Philadelphia in the Romantic Age of Lithography*. Philadelphia: Historical Society of Pennsylvania, 1958.

A Walk on the Wild Side: The Wissahickon Creek, 1800–1940. Philadelphia: Library Company, [1993].

[Waln, Robert]. *The Hermit in America on a Visit to Philadelphia*. Philadelphia: M. Thomas, 1819.

Warner, Sam Bass Jr. *The Private City: Philadelphia in Three Periods of Its Growth*. Philadelphia: University of Pennsylvania Press, 1968.

Watkin, Edward W. *A Trip to the United States and Canada*. London: W. H. Smith, 1852.

Watson, John F. *Annals of Philadelphia and Pennsylvania*. Philadelphia: Leary, Stuart, 1927.

Webb, Beatrice. *American Diary, 1898*. Ed. David A. Shannon. Madison: University of Wisconsin Press, 1963.

Weigley, Russell F., ed. *Philadelphia: A 300-Year History*. New York: Norton, 1982.

Welby, Adlard. *A Visit to North America*. London: J. Drury, 1821.

Weld, Charles Richard. *A Vacation Tour in the United States and Canada*. London: Longman, Brown, Green, 1855.

Weston, Richard. *A Visit to the United States and Canada in 1833 with the View of Settling in America*. Edinburgh: Richard Weston and Sons, 1836.

Wharton, Anne H. "The Philadelphia Wistar Parties." *Lippincott's Magazine* 39 (June 1887): 978–88.

White, Charles Henry. "Philadelphia." *Harper's* 113 (June 1906): 42–52.

White, D. Fetedoff. "A Russian Sketches Philadelphia, 1811–1831." *PMHB* 75 (January 1951): 3–24.

White, Morton, and Lucia White. *The Intellectual and the City*. Cambridge, Mass.: Harvard University Press, 1962.

Whitman, Walt. *Prose Works 1892, Vol. I, Specimen Days*. Ed. Floyd Stovall. New York: New York University Press, 1963.

Whyte, William H. *City: Rediscovering the Center*. New York: Doubleday, 1988.

Wildes, Harry Emerson. *William Penn*. New York: Macmillan, 1974.

Winpenny, Thomas R. "The Nefarious Philadelphia Plan and Urban America: A Reconsideration." *PMHB* 101 (January 1977): 103–13.

Wolf, Edwin, II. "The Origins of Philadelphia's Self-Depreciation, 1820–1920." *PMHB* 104 (January 1980): 58–73.

Wortley, Lady Emaline Stuart. *Travels in the United States Etc. during 1849 and 1850*. 3 vols. London: Richard Bentley, 1851.

Wortley, Victoria Stuart. *A Young Traveller's Journal of a Year in North and South America during the Year 1850*. London: Bosworth, 1852.

The WPA Guide to Philadelphia. 1937. Reprint, Philadelphia: University of Pennsylvania Press, 1988.

Yardley, Jonathan. *States of Mind: A Personal Journey through the Mid-Atlantic*. New York: Villard, 1993.

Zachary, Alan M. "Social Disorder and the Philadelphia Elite before Jackson." *PMHB* 99 (July 1975): 288–308.

Index